THE ULTIMATE
JUICE BOOK

THE ULTIMATE
JUICE BOOK

OVER 300 JUICES, SHAKES & SMOOTHIES TO
BOOST YOUR MIND, MOOD & HEALTH

WITH AN INTRODUCTION BY **WENDY SWEETSER**

STERLING
New York

STERLING
New York

An Imprint of Sterling Publishing
387 Park Avenue South
New York, NY 10016

Consumer advisory: Consuming raw eggs may increase the risk of food-borne illness

Introduction: Wendy Sweetser
Recipes: Kate Kamil, Catrine Mannerup and Stockfood Ltd
Detox program: Vibeke Klementsen
Project Editor: Helena Caldon
Art Director: Geoff Borin
Publisher: James Tavendale

ISBN 978-1-4549-1034-3

Distributed in Canada by Sterling Publishing
c/o Canadian Manda Group, 165 Dufferin Street
Toronto, Ontario, Canada M6K 3H6
Distributed in the United Kingdom by GMC Distribution Services
Castle Place, 166 High Street, Lewes, East Sussex, England BN7 1XU
Distributed in Australia by Capricorn Link (Australia) Pty. Ltd.
P.O. Box 704, Windsor, NSW 2756, Australia

For information about custom editions, special sales, and premium and corporate purchases, please
contact Sterling Special Sales at 800-805-5489 or specialsales@sterlingpublishing.com.

Manufactured in China

2 4 6 8 10 9 7 5 3 1

www.sterlingpublishing.com

contents

introduction

Pour a long, cool glass of a juice, smoothie, or shake that you've made yourself and, before you've even taken the first mouthful, just looking at it will make you feel good.

The great advantage of homemade drinks over commercially prepared ones is that you can decide what goes into them and you can vary the ingredients according to personal taste.

If you prefer sharper flavors, a squeeze of lemon or lime juice will add a citrusy tang, or if something sweeter suits you, pop in a few extra strawberries, a ripe peach, or a larger slice of melon. On days when you want to detox but can't face an overload of the earthy taste of beets or cabbage in your morning juice or smoothie, try disguising their flavors by teaming them with some more palatable ingredients like carrots and apples.

As about 95% of the nutrients in fruit and vegetables are found in their juice, the liquid extracted from them forms an important part of a healthy diet, making juices an easy, and highly enjoyable, way of upping your intake of body-boosting minerals and vitamins. However, when the juice is extracted from fruits and vegetables, the fiber content is considerably reduced, meaning the nutritional benefits are lower than if you had eaten the whole fruit. For this reason a juice only counts as one of your recommended five-a-day, regardless of how many different types of fruit and vegetables are used to make it or how many glasses of it you drink.

On the other hand, smoothies and shakes that are made by crushing whole fruit or vegetables with juices, dairy products, or other ingredients, have higher levels of carbohydrate, fiber, energy, sugars, and vitamin C than pure juices so are equal to two portions of your daily allowance, since they contain the pulp as well as the juice of the fruit or vegetable.

Recently, it has become increasingly common for scare stories to appear in our newspapers and magazines that juicing might actually be bad for us. The argument goes that the process of extracting the liquid and nutrients from a fruit or vegetable has the effect of discarding their tough fibers which aid digestion. Smoothies also haven't escaped the reproving eye of the health police, who point out that they can greatly increase the amount of sugar we consume. It is true that too much sugar and acid can wear away the enamel on our teeth and an over-consumption of sugar increases our risk of developing type 2 diabetes in later life but, as with most things we eat and drink, the key to a balanced diet is moderation and the number of juices and smoothies we consume is no exception.

On the positive side, a glass of a homemade juice or smoothie will always be fresher than any standard commercially-made equivalent, it will be better for you and is there to be enjoyed, either by kick-starting your day or as a pick-me-up when you're on the go. Opening a carton of bought juice simply doesn't compare with the anticipation you feel when pour out a drink you've just made, as you know immediately how good it's going to taste.

juices

juicing machines

There is a wide range of juicers on the market from basic machines to the expensive heavy-duty pulverizers seen in juice bars. The simplest and cheapest version is an old-fashioned lemon squeezer or citrus press. If you only want to make orange juice or need lemon juice to add to a drink, this will extract more juice from a citrus fruit than any other machine.

Most juicers are "centrifugal extractors," where fruit and vegetables are pushed down a feeder tube into a spinning basket with a powerful grater at the base. The pulp is shredded and trapped while the juice pours out the side and is collected in a jug.

The more expensive the machine the bigger its motor will be, so more juice is extracted and it is better equipped to cope with tough, fibrous fruit and vegetables. Less-powerful juicers may have an automatic cut-out that kicks in when the machine is put under excess stress from too many tough ingredients being pushed down the feeder tube at one time. When juicing particularly fibrous ingredients like pumpkins, sprouts, cabbage, or raw beets in any kind of machine, it helps to chop them into small pieces first.

When buying a juicer, always follow the manufacturer's safety instructions carefully when assembling, using, dismantling, and cleaning the machine.

making juices

As most nutrients in fruits and vegetables are found just under the skin, a juice will be healthier if the skin is left on. All produce—whether organic or non-organic—must first be washed thoroughly in

warm water, but only remove the skin if it is very hard. For example, watermelons have thin smooth skins that contain lots of juice so it can be left on, whereas galia or canteloupe melons have tough, dry skins that are likely to jam a juicer if it is not cut away first.

Hard pits in fruits like plums, peaches, avocadoes, or apricots, and any tough stalks, must be removed, but softer, non-edible parts like apple cores, melon seeds, and celery leaves can all be left in. Citrus fruits should always be peeled, unless they are being squeezed in a citrus press, as their rind will add a bitter taste if put through a juicer. As the pith of a citrus fruit contains valuable nutrients, only cut away and discard the thin outer zest using a vegetable peeler, leaving the pith attached to the flesh.

Before juicing, cut prepared fruits and vegetables into slices or chunks small enough for them to fit comfortably down the feeder tube of the juicer. Virtually any fruit or vegetable can be juiced, the yield of liquid produced will vary according to the percentage of juice they contain. However, if adding bananas to a juice it is best to liquidize the banana in a blender with the finished juice rather than feed it through the juicer and watch it disappear immediately into the pulp to be discarded.

When adding fruit and vegetables to the juicer, push the pieces down the feeder tube using the food pusher—never your hands—to extract the maximum juice. If you cannot process all the ingredients in one go, switch off the machine and let the mechanism slow down and stop before you lift the food pusher to add the remainder.

smoothies and shakes

equipment needed

A juice machine is not needed to make smoothies, where the whole fruit is blended in a liquidizer rather than just the juice being extracted. However, if a smoothie recipe requires orange, apple, pineapple, grapefruit, or other juices to be blended with whole fruit, these can first be made in a juicer.

Shakes are made in different ways, with some being blended in a liquidizer, others shaken in a sealed container like a cocktail shaker or screw-top jar, or the ingredients simply stirred or muddled together.

making smoothies and shakes

Fruits and vegetables need to be peeled and any pips, cores, and seeds removed. It is particularly important to remove the seeds and the skins from tomatoes as if these are blitzed with the rest of the pulp they will give the finished drink a bitter taste.

Whether or not to strain a smoothie or shake is very much down to personal taste. Although pips, pits, and skins can be removed from the majority of fruits, it's not possible to do this with soft fruits such as raspberries and blackberries, nor is it practical to try and skin small fruits like cherries, grapes, and blueberries. When blended, the skins of these fruits and berry pips will not break down completely but will remain as flecks through the drink, so you might prefer to strain it.

As both the pulp and the juice are blended together, smoothies and shakes are thicker than a juice so, if they are too thick, dilute them to the desired consistency with mineral water, milk, or extra fruit juice.

how long will juices, smoothies and shakes keep for?

All juices or blended drinks are best drunk freshly made since the longer they are stored the more vitamins are lost and they will start to oxidize when exposed to the air. This oxidation process also causes drinks containing apples, pears, avocadoes, and bananas to discolour. Oxidation can be slowed by adding lemon juice to a drink.

If making larger quantities of drinks, prepare them ahead as near to the start time as practicable and store in the fridge or a cool place until needed. If the drinks start to separate, give them a good stir before pouring into glasses. They can also be served with swizzle sticks of melon, pepper, carrot, cucumber, or celery for drinkers to stir them up themselves. Some drinks thicken up on standing, so let them down to the desired consistency with a little mineral water or extra juice just before serving.

the health benefits of the main fruits and vegetbles used in this book

apples

Apples have been around since the dawn of time and two a day are said to lower cholesterol, as well as keep the doctor away. The malic and tartaric acids found in apples aid digestion by breaking down fat in the body.

apricots

A powerhouse of good things, apricots don't just contain valuable levels of vitamins A, C, and E but also potassium, iron, beta carotene, and a useful amount of fiber.

avocadoes

Avocadoes contain all 18 essential amino acids that are the building blocks needed by the body for protein and to build muscle tissue. More easily absorbed than other protein sources, such as red meat, avocadoes also contain fiber and are an excellent source of carotenoids.

bananas

One of nature's superfoods, bananas are a great source of potassium that helps keep blood pressure low. They also provide a sustained burst of energy that boosts brainpower so, if eaten for breakfast, help keep us going until it is time for lunch.

beets

Full of minerals and vitamins to cleanse the blood and help fight fatigue, beets also give juices a vivid jewel-like hue. They have a strong, earthy flavor so, if this is not to your taste, try partnering them with sweeter produce like apples, pears, and carrots.

blueberries

Another of nature's most powerful health foods, blueberries protect the cells in the body by helping to neutralize dangerous free radicals and act as a natural booster for blood vessels.

carrots

Our grandmothers always told us if we ate our carrots we'd be able to see in the dark—and they were right! One large carrot contains enough beta-carotene for our metabolisms to convert into an entire day's requirement of vitamin A—the nutrient for healthy, bright eyes.

figs

If Adam and Eve used fig leaves to preserve their modesty, presumably these luscious fruits featured regularly on the menu in the Garden of Eden. As with many ancient fruits, figs have long been prized for being part-medicine/part-sheer indulgence as they are a valuable source of fiber, iron, and potassium as well as being acknowledged across Asia as one of nature's great aphrodisiacs.

grapes

Grapes come in different sizes, can be red, black, or green in colour and have pips or be seedless. Red grapes have higher levels of antioxidants than green grapes but all contribute a useful amount of vitamin A to our diet, which is important for good eyesight, growth, healthy tissues, and strong bones.

kiwi fruit

Asked to name good sources of vitamin C, oranges would come high on most peoples' lists but, weight for weight, kiwi fruit contain more vitamins than oranges. Just one of these small, hairy, nutritional powerhouses provides all our recommended daily intake of vitamin C.

melons

Small melons such as galia and ogen are fragrant and juicy when ripe but although they provide some vitamin A and C, their main contribution to a drink is to add a natural sweetness. Watermelons, on the other hand, contain powerful antioxidants, plus concentrated amounts of vitamins A and C.

oranges

Oranges are a rich source of vitamin C, plus if they are blitzed to make a smoothie rather than juiced, they retain their soluble fiber, which slows down the rate at which sugar is absorbed by the body. Florida's climate of hot sun followed by sudden downpours of heavy rain, produces fruit with a thinner rind and more juice than oranges from Jaffa or Spain so will feel heavy for their size.

papaya

This tropical fruit can vary wildly in shape and size from small, yellow pears to long, green giants the size of vegetable marrows. Whatever their appearance, all papayas are a rich source of vitamins A and C, plus calcium for strong bones.

pears

Although not in the premier league of nutrient-rich fruits, pears are still a good source of soluble fiber, vitamin C, and potassium.

pineapple

Pineapple might have only half the vitamin C of citrus fruits and less vitamin A than papaya but it still provides a useful amount of dietary fiber.

pomegranates

Having languished for centuries in the culinary wilderness, pomegranates are now a star turn, the leathery-skinned fruit with its red crunchy seeds being hailed as a superfood that's packed with antioxidants to protect the body from free radicals.

raspberries

Raspberries might be prized as a true taste of summer but their nutrient content is valuable too as they contain sizeable amounts of iron, vitamin C, fiber, and flavonoids that are potent antioxidants.

spinach

While it might not give you muscles to rival those of Popeye, spinach is definitely a body builder. Full of vitamin C, iron, and folate to build healthy blood cells and help prevent anaemia, the rich green leaves also contain oxygen-boosting chlorophyll. However, spinach is also high in oxalic acid which, if absorbed in large quantities, affects the body's ability to absorb calcium, so the leaves need to be mixed with other fruits and vegetables rather than juiced on their own.

strawberries

The only fruit to have their seeds on the outside, strawberries contain high levels of vitamin C and soluble fiber that helps break down "bad" cholesterol in the body.

tomatoes

The vegetable that's really a fruit. Rich in antioxidants such as vitamin C, flavonoids, and the carotenoid lycopene, tomatoes can help protect against heart disease and some cancers.

some of the more unusual ingredients used

acai berries
These small purple berries of the acai (pronounced "ah-sai-ee") tree, native to the Amazonian rainforest, contain jaw-dropping amounts of antioxidants plus vitamins, calcium, iron, and amino acids. Definitely not a berry that needs to justify its superfood credentials.

aloe vera
The health benefits of aloe vera juice were first recognised by the Ancient Egyptians 5,000 years ago. Said to help weight loss and aid digestion, it also boosts the immune system.

flaxseeds
Also called linseed, flax is one of the oldest fiber crops in the world, having been cultivated by the Ancient Egyptians and Chinese. The small seeds of the plant are rich in fiber, minerals, and vitamins and contain two essential fatty acids.

lily flower
Also called "oriental lily," these flowers help regulate the heart so it beats efficiently. They make a popular and soothing tea in Asian countries.

sea buckthorn

Eat just a few berries of sea buckthorn and you'll benefit by imbibing as much vitamin C as if you had eaten 8 oranges. The orange berries have a unique, tart flavor and are rich in omega 3 and 6 fatty acids that help prevent, among other things, heart disease and cancer.

spirulina

A form of chlorophyll available as a dense green powder, spirulina has a strong flavor that needs balancing with sweeter fruits and vegetables. Mix the powder with a little juice before adding it to a drink. Spirulina is best used to make a juice that is already green as it will tint most other juices a rather unappetising shade of khaki.

get juicing!

You may be new to juicing and making smoothies, or you may think you already know your favorite flavor combination, but read on. Here are 300 recipes to tickle your tastebuds and get you to try fruits and vegetables you might otherwise never have included in your diet. They have all been tried and tested to be healthy, nutritious, and delicious. If you feel really inspired by how good these drinks make you feel, why not try the three-day detox, complete with tasty and satisfying recipes, which will purify your body and help you lose weight too.

So what are you waiting for? Get out your juicer and your blender and make a difference to your diet today.

juices

2 **cucumbers**

8 **apples**, roughly chopped

apple and cucumber juice

1 Cut several slices from the end of one of the cucumbers and set aside to decorate.

2 Peel the remaining cucumbers, cut them in half lengthways and remove the seeds. Roughly chop the cucumber flesh.

3 Pass the chopped cucumbers and apples through a vegetable juicer and serve the juice in glasses decorated with the cucumber slices.

9 oz ripe **strawberries**, roughly chopped, plus 4 to decorate

4 tbsp **sugar**

juice of 1 **lemon**

8 **basil leaves**, finely chopped, plus 8 to decorate

crushed ice

soda water

strawberry and basil crush

1 Place the chopped strawberries in a bowl and mix in the sugar. Set aside for 20 minutes, then press the fruit through a fine sieve.

2 Mix the strawberry juice with the lemon juice and chopped basil and pour into 4 cocktail glasses filled with crushed ice.

3 Add a splash of soda water and decorate the glasses with the whole strawberries and basil leaves.

7 tbsp **grenadine**

2 cups **grapefruit juice**

juice of 1 **lemon**

ice cubes

grenadine, grapefruit, and lemon juice

1 Mix all the ingredients together and pour into 4 glasses.

2 Add a couple of ice cubes and serve immediately.

1½ cups **oat milk**

1½ cups **orange juice**

1 **banana**, roughly chopped

7 tbsp **sea buckthorn berry juice**

orange and sea buckthorn berry drink

1 Place all the ingredients in a blender and blend until smooth.

2 Pour into 4 glasses and serve immediately.

16 oz **white grapes**

8 **kiwi fruit**, peeled and roughly chopped

kiwi fruit and grape juice

1 Pass the grapes and kiwi fruit through a vegetable juicer.

2 Press the juice through a fine sieve to get rid of any pips or skin and pour into 4 glasses.

2 in **fresh ginger**, peeled

1 **lemon**, peeled

1 cup **elderflower cordial**

3 cups **water**

ice cubes

citrus slices, to decorate

mint leaves, to decorate

elderflower and ginger cooler

1 Put the ginger and lemon into a juicer together.

2 Mix the elderflower cordial into the ginger and lemon juice and pour into 4 glasses.

3 Top up each glass with water and ice and decorate with slices of your favorite citrus fruits and mint leaves.

MAKES 4 servings   **PREP TIME** 10 min   **DIFFICULTY** easy

2 **beets**, peeled and cut in half

2 **oranges**, peeled

2 in **fresh ginger**, peeled

orange, beets, and ginger energizer

1 Put all the ingredients in the juicer, adding the ginger pieces in between each orange.

2 Serve in small glasses.

4½ oz **raspberries**

2½ oz **sugar**

juice and zest of 2 **limes**

¼ cup **water**

lime slices, to decorate

raspberry lime rickey

1 Place the raspberries, sugar, lime juice and zest, and water in a small pan and heat very gently, stirring occasionally, until the sugar has dissolved.

2 Simmer for 5 minutes then strain through a fine sieve and let the syrup cool.

3 To serve, dilute about 1 cup of the syrup with still or sparkling water and serve over ice in glasses decorated with the lime slices.

5 ripe **nectarines**

4 **blood oranges**

mint leaves

blood orange and nectarine juice

1 Cut one of the nectarines into thin slices, thread them evenly onto 4 cocktail sticks and set aside.

2 Cut 2 slices from one of the blood oranges, cut these in half and set aside for the decoration. Juice the remaining oranges.

3 Peel the remaining nectarines and remove the pits. Roughly chop the flesh, place in a blender and blend until smooth.

4 Mix the orange juice with the nectarine pulp and serve in glasses. Decorate with the nectarine and orange slices and the mint leaves.

1 ripe **papaya**, peeled, seeds removed and roughly chopped

juice of 1 **lime**

2 tbsp **runny honey**

3 cups **apple juice**

16 **ice cubes**

lemon slices, to decorate

papaya and apple crush

1 Place the chopped papaya, lime juice, honey, apple juice, and ice in a blender and blend until the ice is roughly crushed.

2 Pour into glasses and decorate with the lemon slices.

1 small **coconut**, shell removed

sugar, to taste

½ small **watermelon**, peeled and seeds removed

1 small **honeydew melon**, peeled and seeds removed

watermelon, honeydew melon, and coconut drink

1 Cut the coconut in half, reserving the juice, then roughly chop the flesh.

2 Place the coconut flesh in a blender with 2 cups hot water and blend until smooth. Pass the coconut pulp through a fine sieve, mix with the coconut juice and sweeten to taste with the sugar. Place the coconut drink in the fridge until ready to serve.

3 Place the watermelon flesh in a blender and blend until smooth. Pass through a fine sieve and set aside.

4 Place the melon in a blender, add 1 cup cold water and blend until smooth.

5 Pour the drinks into chilled glasses and serve.

6 ripe **persimmons**

14 oz **tinned lychees**

2 tbsp **honey**

juice of 2 **limes**

2 sprigs **mint**, roughly chopped

crushed ice, to serve

Japanese persimmon and lychee drink

1 Cut the persimmons in half and scoop out the flesh.

2 Place the persimmons in a blender with the lychees and their juice and blend until smooth. Add the honey, lime juice, and chopped mint and mix well.

3 Pour the juice into a jug filled with crushed ice and serve immediately.

½ **pineapple**, peeled and roughly chopped, plus 4 slices to decorate

2 handfuls **blackberries**

3–4 **green apples**

blackberry, apple, and pineapple juice

1 Put all the ingredients in the juicer together.

2 Pour the juice into 4 glasses and decorate with pineapple slices.

6–7 **sweet apples**

1 ½ handfuls **parsley**

6–7 **celery stalks**, plus **sprigs / leaves** to decorate

1 **lemon**, peeled

parsley, apple, and celery juice

1 Put all the ingredients in the juicer.

2 Pour into 4 glasses and decorate with the celery sprigs or leaves.

2 large **carrots**

1 large **mango**, peeled, pits removed, and flesh roughly chopped

2 cups **orange juice**

ice cubes

mint leaves (optional), to decorate

carrot, mango, and orange juice

1 Pass the carrots through a vegetable juicer.

2 Place the carrot juice in a blender with the chopped mango and orange juice. Blend until smooth and serve over ice, decorated with mint leaves, if desired.

MAKES 4 servings   **PREP TIME** 20 min   **DIFFICULTY** easy

2 tbsp **assam tea leaves**

2 cups **boiling water**

4 tbsp **brown sugar crystals**

juice of 1 **lemon**

juice of 2 **oranges**

8 **star anise**

8 **mint leaves**

½ **orange**, sliced

½ **lemon**, sliced

anti-flu punch

1 Put the tea leaves in a heatproof jug and pour over the boiling water. Set aside to brew for 10 minutes.

2 Strain the tea into a small pan and add the remaining ingredients. Heat gently, stirring occasionally, until the sugar has dissolved, then pour into 4 heatproof glasses and serve immediately.

6 large ripe **tomatoes**

½ **watermelon**, peeled, seeds removed, and roughly chopped

2 tbsp **white wine vinegar**

8 **ice cubes**

lime slices, to decorate

tomato and watermelon drink

1 Roughly chop the tomatoes and pulp the flesh using a stick blender. Pass the pulp through a fine sieve.

2 Place the tomato juice in a blender with the chopped watermelon and add the vinegar and ice cubes. Blend until smooth and pour into glasses.

3 Serve decorated with the lime slices.

1 small **pineapple**, peeled and core removed
½ **canteloupe melon**, peeled, seeds removed, and roughly chopped
4 tbsp **plain yogurt**
1 cup **water**
2 tbsp **honey**

pineapple and cantaloupe melon drink

1 Roughly chop the pineapple flesh and place in a blender with the melon, yogurt, water, and honey.

2 Blend until smooth, adding a little more water if necessary, then pour into 4 glasses and serve.

1 small **papaya**

4 slices **apple**

3 cups **apple juice**

juice of 1 **lime**

fruity summer drink

1 Cut 8 small slices from the papaya, thread onto cocktail sticks with the apple slices and set aside for the decoration.

2 Peel the remaining fruit, remove the seeds and roughly chop the flesh. Place the papaya flesh in a blender with the apple juice and lime juice and blend until smooth.

3 Pour into 4 glasses and serve decorated with the papaya and apple slices.

8 **kiwis**, peeled

1½ **cantaloupe melons**, peeled

1 handful **basil leaves**

1 **lemon**, peeled

kiwi, melon, and basil juice

1 Put all the ingredients in a juicer, adding the basil leaves between the kiwis and melons.

2 Pour into 4 glasses.

4 **apples**, halved

3 **oranges**, peeled

1 ½ **fennel bulbs**, cut in quarters

apple, orange, and fennel juice

1 Put all the ingredients in a juicer, adding the fennel between the apples and oranges.

2 Pour into 4 glasses.

8 ripe **peaches**, peeled and pits removed

juice of 2 **limes**, plus 4 slices to decorate

½ cup **water**

2 tbsp **sugar**

peach and lime drink

1 Roughly chop the peach flesh and place in a blender with the lime juice, water, and sugar.

2 Blend until smooth then pass through a sieve and pour the juice into glasses. Serve decorated with the lime slices.

3 cups **pineapple juice**

1 cup **orange juice**

juice of 1 **lime**

ice cubes

pineapple slices, to decorate

pineapple cocktail

1 Mix all the juices together and pour into glasses over ice.

2 Decorate with the pineapple slices and serve.

4 **oranges**

1 small **papaya**, peeled, seeds removed, and flesh roughly chopped

juice of 1 **lime**

ice cubes

mint sprigs, to decorate

orange and papaya drink

1 Cut 4 long strips of peel from the oranges, twist them into spirals around the handle of a wooden spoon and set aside for the decoration.

2 Juice the oranges and place the juice in a blender with the chopped papaya and lime juice. Blend until smooth then pass through a fine sieve.

3 Pour into glasses over ice and serve decorated with the orange peel spirals and mint leaves.

4 **apples**, peeled, cored, and roughly chopped

18 oz **blackberries**

2 **pears**, peeled, cored, and roughly chopped

4 tbsp **sugar**

juice of 1 **lemon**

apple, blackberry, and pear juice

1 Place the apples, blackberries, and pears in a small pan with the sugar. Cook very gently until the fruit is soft.

2 Pass the fruit mixture through a fine sieve, mix in the lemon juice and chill for 1 hour before serving.

8 ripe **pears**, peeled, cored, and roughly chopped

juice of 2 **limes**

pear and lime juice

1 Pass the pears through a vegetable juicer and mix with the lime juice. Serve immediately.

9 oz **dried apricots**

2 cups **apple juice**

1 cup **water**

apricot juice

1 Place the apricots in a bowl with the apple juice and water and leave to soak for 1 hour.

2 Transfer to a blender and blend until smooth. Pass through a sieve and serve.

2 cups **lychee juice**, from a carton

juice of 3 **limes**

ice cubes

1 cup **soda water**

lychee sparkler

1 Mix together the lychee and lime juices and pour over ice cubes in 4 tall glasses. Top up with soda.

10 medium-sized **ripe tomatoes**, halved

8 stalks **celery** incl. leaves

1 **red pepper**, deeseeded and chopped

1 **cucumber**, halved

½ **red chili**, use your favorite variety

1 **lemon**, peeled

1 tsp **sugar**

1½ tsp **salt**

ground black pepper

celery leaves, to garnish

spicy tomato juice

1 Put all the fruit and veg in the juicer, adding the chili between the tomatoes and cucumbers.

2 Pour into 4 glasses, mix in the sugar, salt, and pepper and stir. Garnish with celery leaves.

3 cups **pink grapefruit juice**
juice of 1 **lemon**, plus 4 slices
4 tsp **grenadine**
ice cubes

pink grapefruit juice

1 Mix together the grapefruit juice, lemon juice, and grenadine.

2 Place one lemon slice in each glass, fill with ice cubes and top up with the juice mixture.

seeds from 1 **pomegranate**

crushed ice

1 cup **pomegranate juice**

juice of 4 **oranges**

orange and pomegranate juice

1 Place the pomegranate seeds in the bottom of 4 glasses.

2 Fill each glass with crushed ice and pour over the pomegranate juice.

3 Add the orange juice and serve immediately.

4 **eating apples**, peeled and cored
2 sticks **celery**, finely chopped
2 cups **plain yogurt**
parsley sprigs, to decorate
apple slices, to decorate

apple and celery juice

1 Finely chop the apples and blend with the celery and yogurt.

2 Pour into 4 glasses and garnish with the parsley sprigs and apple slices.

¼ **white cabbage**, roughly chopped

6 **apples**, halved

4 large handfuls **fresh spinach**, washed

2 **bananas**, chopped

ice cubes

cabbage, banana, apple, and spinach juice

1 Put the cabbage, apples, and spinach in the juicer, adding the spinach leaves in between the cabbage and apples.

2 Pour the juice into a mixer, add the bananas and ice cubes and blend till you have a smooth texture.

¼ **pineapple**, peeled, cored, and finely chopped

4 **passion fruits**, pulp only

1 **orange**, peeled and segmented

1 **banana**, thinly sliced

2 cups **red wine** or grape juice
if you prefer a non-alcoholic drink

6 drops **angostura bitters**

1 cup **orange juice**, fresh or shop-bought

1 stick **cinnamon**

Zanzibar-style sangria

1 Mix all the ingredients together in a large pitcher, cover and refrigerate for 2 hours before serving.

2 Pour equal amounts of fruit and liquid into glasses, removing the cinnamon stick, and serve with a spoon.

3 cups **plain yogurt**

2 handfuls chopped **mixed herb leaves**—parsley, mint, cilantro

4 **ice cubes**

salt and freshly ground black pepper

herb power drink

1 Blend the yogurt with the herbs and ice cubes and season with salt and pepper.

2 Pour into glasses and serve immediately.

2 large **cucumbers**

2 cups **plain yogurt**

salt and freshly ground black pepper

savory cucumber drink

1 Using a vegetable peeler, cut 4 thin slices of cucumber lengthways and thread them onto long wooden skewers.

2 Peel the remaining cucumbers and roughly chop. Blend the chopped cucumber with the yogurt until smooth then pass through a sieve and season to taste with salt and pepper.

3 Serve in glasses with the skewered cucumber slices.

16 oz **black radish**, peeled and roughly chopped

2 handfuls chopped **mixed herbs**—parsley, mint, cilantro

1 cup **apple juice**

juice of 1 **lemon**

mint sprigs, to garnish

radish and herb cocktail

1 Blend the radish with the herbs, apple juice, and lemon juice.

2 Pour into glasses and serve garnished with the mint sprigs.

1 small **pineapple**

1 medium **papaya**

2 cups **plain yogurt**

ice cubes

1 **starfruit**, thinly sliced

mint sprigs

papaya and pineapple with starfruit and mint

1 Peel, core, and roughly chop the pineapple.

2 Peel the papaya and remove the seeds, reserving a few for the decoration. Roughly chop the flesh.

3 Blend the pineapple and papaya with the yogurt until smooth then pour into glasses filled with ice.

4 Decorate with starfruit slices, mint sprigs, and the reserved papaya seeds.

1 **cucumber**, chopped

2 ripe **avocados**, quartered

2 tsp **spirulina powder**

juice of 1 **lime**

1 **spring onion**, chopped

2 sprigs fresh **cilantro**

dash **chili sauce**

spirulina, cucumber, and avocado drink

1 Put the cucumber into a blender.

2 Peel the avocados, remove the flesh from the pits and add to the blender with the spirulina powder, lime juice, spring onion, cilantro, and chili sauce.

3 Add 2 cups cold water and blend everything together. Pour into 4 glasses and serve.

½ **pineapple**, peeled and halved

1½ **cucumbers**, halved

1½ **oranges**, peeled

½ **red chili**, use your favorite variety

pineapple, cucumber, and red chili juice

1 Put all the ingredients in the juicer, adding the chili between the pineapple and cucumbers.

2 Pour into 4 glasses.

MAKES 4 servings   PREP TIME 5 min   DIFFICULTY easy

2 handfuls **green grapes**
1½ handfuls **raspberries**
1 **cucumber**
1 in **fresh ginger**, peeled

grape, raspberry, and ginger zinger

1 Put all the ingredients in the juicer, adding the ginger between the grapes and cucumber.

2 Pour into 4 glasses.

HOME
MADE

12 cups **raspberries**

water

sugar, to taste

lemon juice, to taste

homemade raspberry juice

1 Put the raspberries in a large pan and add just enough water to cover.

2 Bring to a boil, stirring, then reduce the heat and simmer for 10 minutes. Crush the fruit well to release the juices. Add sugar and lemon juice to taste.

3 Ladle the fruit and juices into a scalded jelly bag set above a bowl. Leave the juice to strain through the jelly bag, squeezing occasionally to extract as much juice as possible.

4 Pour into sterilized bottles to within ½ in of the top and seal tightly.

5 **dried lily flowers**, softened in 2 tbsp hot water for 30 minutes

juice of 4 **oranges**

1 tbsp **maple syrup**

¼ tsp **cinnamon**

1 pinch **ground cloves**

1¼ in **fresh ginger**, peeled and grated

lily flower and orange drink

1 Mix all the ingredients together with 3 cups water.

2 Allow to steep for 30 minutes then pass through a sieve and pour into glasses.

4 large **oranges**

juice of 1 **lemon**

3 tbsp **honey**

2 sprigs **thyme**

ice cubes

orange punch with thyme

1 Using a zester, carefully remove the zest from the oranges in one thread and wrap it around the handle of a wooden spoon to form spirals. Set aside.

2 Squeeze the oranges and place in a small saucepan with the lemon juice, honey, and thyme. Heat gently until the honey has dissolved then strain through a fine sieve and place in the fridge to chill for 30 minutes.

3 Serve the punch over ice and decorate with the zest spirals.

9 oz **cherries**

juice of 1 **lemon**

2 tbsp **sugar**

12 **basil leaves**, roughly torn

ice cubes

3 cups **lemonade**

cherry and basil spritzer

1 Reserve 4 cherries for the decoration. Remove the pits from the remaining cherries and place half in a small pan with the lemon juice and sugar.

2 Cook gently over a low heat until the cherries have softened and the sugar has dissolved, then strain through a fine sieve and pour the juice into 4 glasses.

3 Add the remaining pitted cherries and the torn basil leaves, fill the glasses with ice and top with the lemonade.

4 Thread the whole cherries onto 4 straws and serve immediately.

4 large **carrots**, peeled
4 **green apples**
juice from 2 **pink grapefruits**

grapefruit, carrot, and apple juice

1 Cut 4 slices of carrot and set aside.

2 Cut 4 wedges from one of the apples and set aside.

3 Roughly chop the remaining carrots and apples and pass through a juicer. Mix the juice with the grapefruit juice, pour into glasses and decorate with the reserved apple and carrot slices.

3 handfuls **strawberries**, plus extra to decorate

1 **apple**, halved

8 **rhubarb stalks**, halved

4 tbsp **sugar syrup**

ice cubes

1½ cups **soda water**

rhubarb and strawberry cooler

1 Juice the strawberries, apple, and rhubarb and mix the juices with sugar syrup.

2 Put ice in 4 glasses, pour the juice over and top up with soda water.

3 Garnish with the reserved strawberries.

MAKES 4 servings   **PREP TIME** 5 min   **DIFFICULTY** easy

8 **carrots**, peeled
¼ **cabbage head**
6 **oranges**

cabbage, carrot, and orange juice

1 Put all the ingredients in the juicer.

2 Pour into 4 glasses.

16 oz **cooked beets**
3 cups **apple juice**
4 tbsp **sesame seeds**

beet and apple drink

1 Roughly chop the beets and place in a blender with the apple juice and sesame seeds.

2 Blend until smooth and serve in 4 glasses.

16 oz **red currants**

9 oz **raspberries**

9 oz **sugar**

1 cup **water**

fruit and vegetable cocktail

1 Place the red currants and raspberries in a pan and mash them with a fork.

2 Add the sugar and water and heat gently until the sugar has dissolved, stirring from time to time.

3 Strain the cordial through a muslin or very fine sieve and let cool.

4 Serve diluted with equal parts of water, or according to taste.

9 oz **cooked beets**, roughly chopped

2 large **carrots**, roughly chopped

1 cup **apple juice**

carrot and beet juice

1 Pass the beets and carrots through a vegetable juicer.

2 Mix in the apple juice and serve.

2 **apples**, cored and roughly chopped

2 large **carrots**, roughly chopped

2 cups **orange juice**

ice cubes

apple, orange, and carrot juice

1 Pass the apples and carrots through a vegetable juicer and mix with the orange juice.

2 Serve over ice.

3½ oz **spinach**

½ small **honeydew melon**, peeled, seeds removed, and roughly chopped

ice cubes

spinach and melon drink

1 Pass the spinach and melon through a vegetable juicer.

2 Serve in 4 glasses with a few cubes of ice.

5 **oranges**

6 **kiwis**

2 handfuls **spinach**

orange, kiwi, and spinach juice

1 Put all the ingredients in the juicer, adding the spinach between the oranges and kiwis.

2 Pour into 4 glasses.

2 **grapefruits**

1 **lemon**

2 in **fresh ginger**, peeled

4 tbsp **honey**

grapefruit, lemon, honey, and ginger juice

1 Put the grapefruit, lemon, and ginger in a juicer.

2 Pour into 4 glasses and stir the honey into each glass.

8 **apples**, peeled, cored, and roughly chopped
9 oz **cooked beets**, roughly chopped
2 in **fresh ginger**, peeled and sliced
ice cubes

beet, ginger, and apple juice

1 Pass the apples, beets, and ginger through a vegetable juicer.

2 Serve over ice.

2 **red chilies**, seeds removed and roughly chopped

3 cups **buttermilk**

ice cubes

1 tsp **ground cinnamon**

chili and cinnamon drink

1 Place the chilies in a blender with the buttermilk and blend until smooth.

2 Pour into glasses over ice and sprinkle over the cinnamon. Serve immediately.

4 **kumquats**

ice cubes

4 **oranges** or 8 **clementines**

soda water

kumquat and orange juice

1 Slice the kumquats, remove the seeds and place the slices in the bottom of 4 glasses. Gently muddle the fruit with the handle of a wooden spoon to release the juice. Add ice to the top of each glass.

2 Squeeze the oranges or clementines, sieve the juice and pour into the glasses. Top each one with a splash of soda and serve immediately.

juice of 1 **lemon**

juice of 2 **limes**

4 tbsp **sugar**

crushed ice

3 cups **soda water**

2 **kiwi fruit**, peeled and sliced

12 **blackberries**

kiwi fruit and blackberry punch

1 Mix the lemon and lime juices with the sugar and stir until the sugar has dissolved.

2 Divide the mixture between 4 glasses and fill the glasses with crushed ice. Top up with soda water, add the kiwi slices and blackberries, stir, and serve immediately.

4 **apples**

juice of 2 **lemons**

2 tbsp **sugar**

ice cubes

soda water

apple cocktail and lemonade

1 Cut 8 thin slices from one of the apples and set aside for the decoration.

2 Roughly chop the remaining apples and pass through a vegetable juicer.

3 Mix the lemon juice with the sugar and stir until the sugar has dissolved. Add the apple juice and pour into glasses filled with ice.

4 Top with soda water, decorate with the apple slices and serve immediately.

1 cups **dandelion cordial**
½ cup **lime juice**
ice cubes
2 cups **tonic water**

dandelion cooler

1 Mix the cordial and lime juice in the glasses.

2 Add ice cubes and pour in the tonic water.

MAKES 4 servings   PREP TIME 5 min   DIFFICULTY easy

4 **kiwi fruits**, peeled
5 **passion fruits**, pulp only
4 **oranges**

passion fruit, kiwi, and orange juice

1 Put all the ingredients in the juicer, adding the passion fruit between the oranges and kiwis.

2 Pour into 4 glasses.

2 cups **cranberry juice**, chilled

2 cups **clear apple juice**, chilled

8 drops **orange bitters** (optional)

2½ oz **fresh cranberries**

cranberry apple punch

1 Mix together the cranberry and apple juices and stir in the bitters, if using.

2 Pour into 4 glasses, add the cranberries and serve.

juice of 4 **lemons**

juice of 6 **limes**

juice of 2 **oranges**

4 tbsp **honey**

2 in **fresh ginger**, peeled and grated

3 cups **soda water**

lemon, lime and orange slices, to decorate

ice cubes

lemon and lime punch

1 Mix together the citrus juices and pour about 1 cup into a small pan.

2 Add the honey and ginger to the pan and heat gently until the honey has dissolved. Strain into a large bowl and let cool.

3 Pour in the soda water, add the slices of fruit and the ice then ladle into 4 glasses and serve immediately.

5 oz **raspberries**

3½ oz **blackberries**

4 tbsp **sugar**

juice of 2 **limes**, plus slices to decorate

soda water

blackberry and lime drink

1 Set aside a few of the berries and place the rest in a small pan with the sugar and lime juice.

2 Heat very gently until the berries have released their juices and the sugar has dissolved, then strain through a fine sieve and let cool.

3 Divide the juice between 4 glasses, top with soda water and garnish with the reserved berries and the lime slices.

MAKES 4 servings   **PREP TIME** 2 hr   **DIFFICULTY** easy

18 oz **rosehips**, roughly chopped

2¼ cups **sugar**

rosehip syrup

1 Place the rosehips in a large pan with the sugar and 3½ cups of water. Slowly bring to the boil then remove the pan from the heat and allow to steep for 30 minutes.

2 Strain the mixture through a jelly bag or sieve lined with muslin and set the liquid aside. Return the rosehip pulp to the pan with another 4¼ cups of water and bring to the boil. Let it steep for 30 minutes then strain as before.

3 Discard the rosehip pulp and transfer all the strained liquid to a clean pan. Bring to a boil and simmer for 30 minutes or until the syrup is reduced by a half. Let the liquid cool then pour into a sterilized bottle.

4 To serve, dilute the syrup 5 parts to 1 with still or sparkling water.

3 cups **tomato juice**

juice of 1 **lemon**

12 drops **tabasco**

12 drops **Worcestershire sauce**

½ tsp **celery salt**

ice cubes

cucumber wedges, to garnish

lemon slices, to garnish

celery tops, to garnish

guilt-free virgin mary

1 Place the tomato juice, lemon juice, tabasco, Worcestershire sauce, and celery salt in a jug and mix well.

2 Season to taste with salt and pepper then pour into glasses filled with ice. Garnish with the cucumber, lemon slices, and celery tops and serve immediately.

½ **pineapple**, peeled, plus slices to decorate

ice cubes

½ cup **apricot juice**, bottled

2 cups **ginger ale** or ginger beer, as you like

Hawaiian pineapple punch

1 Juice the pineapple.

2 In a large pitcher, add ice cubes and pour over the pineapple and apricot juices.

3 Stir, then pour in the ginger ale/beer.

4 Pour into 4 glasses and garnish with the pineapple slices.

1 bunch **radish**, include the leaves

1 **cucumber**, halved

½ **iceberg lettuce**, halved

1 **lime**, peeled

radish, lettuce, and cucumber juice

1 Put all the ingredients in the juicer, add the lettuce pieces in between the cucumber and radish.

2 Pour into 4 small glasses.

3 cups **sugar**

2 cups **water**

2 handfuls **rose petals**

1¾ oz **vitamin C powder**

8 small **rose buds**

rose syrup

1 Place the sugar and water in a pan and slowly bring to the boil. Stir until the sugar has dissolved, remove from the heat and leave to cool.

2 Add the petals, stir gently, and cover with a lid. Set aside overnight.

3 Strain through a fine sieve, pressing the petals to extract the flavor, then pass the liquid through a jelly bag or a sieve lined with muslin. Gently heat a cup of the liquid with the vitamin C powder until the powder has dissolved then add to the rest of the liquid. Mix well and pour into sterilized bottles.

4 To make the rose ice cubes, place the rose buds in an ice tray, fill with water and freeze for at least 12 hours.

5 To serve, dilute the syrup with 5 parts of still or sparkling water and add the rose ice cubes.

5 oz **strawberries**, hulled and roughly chopped

4 tbsp **sugar**

12 **raspberries**

12 **blackberries**

crushed ice

still or sparkling water

berry cocktail

1 Put the strawberries and sugar in a small pan and heat gently until the strawberry juice begins to run and the sugar has dissolved. Pass the mixture through a fine sieve and let the juice cool.

2 Divide the raspberries and blackberries between 4 glasses and gently crush them with the handle of a wooden spoon.

3 Add the strawberry juice, fill the glasses with crushed ice and top with still or sparkling water. Stir well and serve.

4 large **carrots**, peeled
2 in **fresh ginger**, peeled
juice of 4 **oranges**

carrot and orange juice with ginger

1 Using a vegetable peeler, peel thin strips from one of the carrots about ¼ in wide, knot them loosely and thread onto cocktail sticks for the garnish.

2 Roughly chop the remaining carrot and pass through a vegetable juicer with the ginger.

3 Mix the carrot and ginger juice with the orange juice, pour into glasses and garnish with the carrot strips.

2 cups **grapefruit juice**

½ cup **green tea**, brewed and cooled

4 tbsp **sugar**

juice of 1 **lemon**

ice cubes

soda water

8 **red grapes**, to decorate

Alice in Wonderland cocktail

1 Mix together the grapefruit juice, green tea, sugar, and lemon juice.

2 Pour into 4 glasses, add the ice cubes and top up with soda water.

3 Drop 2 grapes into each glass and serve.

3 **tea bags**

4 cups **boiling water**

4 **peaches**, pits removed and roughly chopped

4 tbsp **sugar**

juice of 1 **lemon**

peach iced tea

1 Make the tea with the tea bags and boiling water and let it steep for 5 minutes.

2 Remove the tea bags, let the tea cool for 10 minutes then pour into a blender and add the other ingredients.

3 Blend until smooth then pass through a sieve and chill for at least 2 hours before serving.

1 large **papaya**, peeled and seeds removed

3 **pears**, halved

½ **lemon**, peeled

1 in **fresh ginger**, peeled

pear, papaya, and ginger zinger

1 Put all the ingredients in the juicer, adding the ginger pieces in between the papaya and pears.

2 Pour into 4 glasses.

6 **plums**, halved and pits removed

1 in **fresh ginger**, peeled

7–8 **apples**, halved

½ **lemon**, peeled

plum, ginger, and apple juice

1 Put all the ingredients in the juicer.

2 Pour into 4 glasses.

1 **Earl Grey tea bag**

1 ⅓ cups **water**

2 cups **cranberry juice**

1 ¼ in **fresh ginger**, peeled and crushed

2 tbsp **sugar**

pinch **nutmeg**

1 **star anise**

1 **lemon**, sliced

3 ½ oz **cranberries**

4 sticks of **cinnamon**

hot cranberry punch

1 Place the tea bag and water in a small pan with the cranberry juice, ginger, sugar, nutmeg, star anise, and lemon slices.

2 Heat very gently until just simmering then remove the pan from the heat and let it steep for 5 minutes.

3 Remove the tea bag from the pan and reheat the liquid gently until simmering. Strain through a fine sieve and pour into 4 glasses.

4 Put a slice of the lemon in each glass, add the cranberries and cinnamon sticks, and serve.

10 **elderflower heads**

4 cups **water**

3¼ cups **sugar**

1 oz **citric acid powder**

2 **lemons**, scrubbed and sliced

elderflower cordial

1 Gently wash the elderflower heads and tie the stalks together in a bundle.

2 Heat the water with the sugar until the water is boiling and the sugar has dissolved, stirring from time to time.

3 Remove the pan from the heat and add the citric acid. Pour the water into a wide-necked jar, add the lemon slices and insert the elderflower heads. Tie the stalks to a spoon and balance it over the neck of the jar.

4 Let it steep for 24 hours, stirring from time to time, then remove the elderflowers and strain the cordial through a fine sieve. Pour into sterilized bottles.

5 To serve, dilute the cordial with 5 parts of still or sparkling water.

4 cups **water**

3¾ cups **sugar**

16 oz **strawberries**, hulled and chopped

1 oz **citric acid powder**

strawberry cordial

1 Place the water in a pan with the sugar and bring to the boil, stirring from time to time.

2 Add the strawberries, simmer for 10 minutes, then stir in the citric acid.

3 Let the mixture cool a little then strain through a fine sieve. Pour into sterilized bottles.

4 To serve, dilute the cordial with 5 parts of still or sparkling water.

MAKES 4 servings   PREP TIME 30 min, plus 24 hr steeping   DIFFICULTY easy

3 **lemons**

2½ oz **sugar**

2 cups **water**

ice cubes

soda water

lemon slices, to decorate

lemonade

1 Juice the lemons, reserving the skins, and place the juice in a pan with the sugar and water.

2 Bring to the boil, stirring from time to time, then remove the pan from the heat and add the lemon skins.

3 Let the mixture steep for 24 hours then strain through a sieve.

4 Serve the lemonade in glasses filled with ice, top up with soda water and add the lemon slices.

2 in **fresh ginger**, peeled and grated

4 tbsp **sugar**

2 cups **water**

mint leaves, to decorate

crushed ice

ginger ale

1 Put the ginger, sugar, and water in a small pan and bring to the boil, stirring all the time.

2 Remove the pan from the heat, let the liquid steep for 8 hours, then strain through a fine sieve.

3 To serve, pour the ginger ale into glasses filled with crushed ice and decorate with mint leaves.

2 handfuls **raspberries**

1 small **melon**, honeydew or cantaloupe, peeled and cut in quarters

1 large **grapefruit**

grapefruit, melon, and raspberry juice

1 Put all the ingredients in the juicer.

2 Pour into 4 glasses.

5 **passion fruit**, pulp only

5 **oranges**, peeled, plus slices to decorate

2 **green apples**, halved

passion fruit and orange juice

1 Put all the ingredients in the juicer.

2 Pour into 4 glasses and decorate with orange slices.

5 oz **strawberries**, roughly chopped

1 cup **apple juice**

1 tsp **balsamic vinegar**

6 **ice cubes**

strawberry leaves, to decorate

strawberry special

1 Place the chopped strawberries, apple juice, balsamic vinegar, and ice cubes in a blender and blend until smooth.

2 Pour into 4 glasses, decorate with the strawberry leaves and serve immediately.

9 oz **cooked beets**

2 large **carrots**

juice of 1 **lemon**

carrot batons, to garnish

beet juice

1 Pass the beets and carrots through a vegetable juicer and mix with the lemon juice.

2 Pour into 4 glasses and serve garnished with the carrot batons.

2 **green tea bags**

2 cups **water**, heated to about 160°F

2 tbsp **honey**

juice of 2 **limes**

crushed ice

mint leaves, to decorate

lime slices, to decorate

green tea and lime punch

1 Put the tea bags in a heatproof pitcher with the water and stir in the honey.

2 Mix in the lime juice and let steep for 5 minutes.

3 Strain through a sieve and let it cool for 1 hour.

4 Pour the punch into glasses filled with crushed ice and decorate with the mint leaves and lime slices.

¾ cup **cream**

juice of 2 **lemons**

2 tbsp **sugar**

ice cubes

soda water

guilt-free gumbo fizz

1 Mix the cream with the lemon juice and sugar and stir until the sugar has dissolved.

2 Pour into 4 glasses filled with ice and top up with soda water. Serve immediately.

4½ oz **strawberries**, roughly chopped

2½ oz **sugar**

juice of 2 **limes**

½ cup **water**

strawberries, to decorate

lime wedges, to decorate

raspberry and lime punch

1 Put the chopped strawberries in a small pan with the sugar, lime juice, and water. Heat very gently, stirring from time to time, until the sugar has dissolved.

2 Strain the mixture through a fine sieve and set aside to cool.

3 To serve, dilute the syrup with water to taste, pour into glasses and decorate with the strawberries and lime wedges.

3 **apples**, halved
ice cubes
1 cup **japanese plum wine**
1 ½ cups **soda water**
mint, to decorate

plum wine and apple cooler

1 Juice the apples.

2 Put ice cubes in 4 glasses and pour in the apple juice and plum wine.

3 Top up with soda water and garnish with mint sprigs.

¼ **celeriac**, peeled and roughly chopped
2 **parsnips**, peeled and halved
2 **beets**, peeled and halved

beets, parsnips, and celeriac juice shots

1 Put all the ingredients in the juicer.

2 Pour into small glasses

3 **red peppers**, seeds removed and roughly chopped

2 **carrots**, roughly chopped

pepper juice

1 Pass the peppers and carrots through a vegetable juicer.

2 Pour into glasses and serve.

4 **carrots**

3 cups **cranberry juice**

6 **ice cubes**

carrot blend

1 Using a vegetable peeler, peel thin strips from one of the carrots to use as the garnish and set aside.

2 Roughly chop the remaining carrots and place in a blender with the cranberry juice and ice cubes.

3 Blend until the carrots are broken up but not completely smooth, pour into glasses and serve with the carrot strips.

5 oz **spinach**, roughly chopped

1 cup **orange juice**

spinach and orange drink

1 Pass the spinach through a vegetable juicer.

2 Mix the spinach juice with the orange juice and pour into small glasses to serve.

¾ cup **sugar**

2 cups **water**

7 oz **red currants**

Swedish red currant juice

1 Place the sugar and water in a pan and heat gently, stirring from time to time, until the sugar has dissolved.

2 Add the red currants, simmer gently for 10 minutes then remove the pan from the heat and let the mixture steep for 8 hours.

3 To serve, pour the mixture into glasses and top up with still or sparkling water.

4 cups **clear apple juice**

1¾ oz **sugar**

2 **lemons**, sliced

20 heads **woodruff flowers**

7 oz **strawberries**, halved

May strawberry punch

1 Heat the apple juice with the sugar and bring to a boil, stirring from time to time.

2 Remove the pan from the heat, add the lemons and woodruff and set aside to steep for 24 hours.

3 Strain the liquid through a jelly bag or sieve lined with muslin into a punch bowl. Add the strawberries and serve.

MAKES 4 servings **PREP TIME** 5 min **DIFFICULTY** easy

2 handfuls **green grapes**

6–7 **tangerines**, peeled

tangerine and grape juice

1 Put all the ingredients in the juicer.

2 Pour into glasses.

3 **pomegranates**, seeds removed
4 **oranges**, peeled
1 **lime**, peeled

pomegranate and orange juice

1 Put all the ingredients in the juicer, adding the pomegranate seeds between the other fruits.

2 Pour into glasses.

14 oz **blackberries**

⅞ cup **water**

3½ oz **sugar**

7 oz **grapes**

juice of 1 **lemon**

mint, to decorate

blackberry and grape juice

1 Place the blackberries in a pan with the water and sugar and heat gently, stirring from time to time, until the sugar has dissolved.

2 Simmer the blackberries gently for 10 minutes then remove the pan from the heat and carefully pour the mixture into a blender.

3 Add the grapes and lemon juice, blend, then strain the mixture through a jelly bag or sieve lined with muslin.

4 Let the juice cool then serve garnished with mint.

1 **Earl Grey tea bag**

1 cup **boiling water**

2 tbsp **honey**

1 tsp **ground mixed spice**

4 **apples**, peeled, cored, and roughly chopped

4 **pears**, peeled, cored, and roughly chopped

juice of 1 **lemon**

2½ oz **dried cranberries**

2½ oz **toasted pinenuts**

cinnamon sticks, to decorate

apple slices, to decorate

apple and pear punch

1 Steep the tea bag in the water for 5 minutes then stir in the honey and spice and stir until the honey has dissolved. Remove the tea bag and discard.

2 Pass the apples and pears through a vegetable juicer and mix in the tea and lemon juice. Set aside to cool for 2 hours.

3 Pour the punch into glasses and add the cranberries and pinenuts. Add the cinnamon sticks and apple slices and serve.

3½ oz **chia seeds**

3 cups **coconut milk**

1 **banana**

juice of 2 **limes**

2 tbsp **honey**

chia seed and lime drink

1 Soak the chia seeds in 1 cup of the coconut milk for 10 minutes.

2 Meanwhile, put the remaining coconut milk in a blender with the banana, lime juice, and honey and blend until smooth.

3 Stir in the chia seed and coconut milk mixture, pour into glasses and serve.

9 oz **cooked beets**

juice of 2 **oranges**

juice of 1 **lemon**

crushed ice

soda water

4 **orange slices**, to garnish

4 **lemon slices**, to garnish

beet and citrus fruit drink

1 Pass the beets through a vegetable juicer and mix the juice with the orange and lemon juices.

2 Fill 4 glasses with crushed ice and pour in the juice mixture.

3 Top up with soda water and garnish each glass with the orange and lemon slices.

MAKES 4 servings   PREP TIME 10 min   DIFFICULTY easy

juice from 4 **pink grapefruit**
juice from 8 **blood oranges**

pink grapefruit juice

1 Mix the juices together and strain through a sieve.

2 Pour into 4 glasses and serve.

1 ½ **pomegranates**, seeds removed and 4 tbsp seeds reserved

½ cup **elderflower cordial**

2 cups **soda water**

pomegranate and elderflower sparkler

1 Juice the pomegranate.

2 Pour the juice and elderflower cordial into glasses, add the reserved pomegranate seeds and top up with soda water.

½ **pineapple**, peeled
3 handfuls **grapes**
ice cubes
pinch of **ground cinnamon**

pineapple and grape juice

1 Juice the pineapple and grapes.

2 Pour over ice and sprinkle some cinnamon on top.

4 handfuls **purple grapes**

3 **apples**

6 **celery stalks**

ice cubes

purple haze juice

1 Put all the ingredients in the juicer.

2 Pour into glasses with ice.

MAKES 4 servings   PREP TIME 15 min   DIFFICULTY medium

1 tbsp **basil seeds** (tukmaria), soaked in cold water for 10 min

juice of 4 **limes**

½ cup **sugar syrup**

still water

ice cubes

lime slices, to decorate

limeade with basil seeds

1 Put the soaked basil seeds in tall glasses, add the lime juice and sugar syrup.

2 Top up with water, ice cubes, and slices of lime.

3 medium-sized **beets**, peeled and chopped in half

3 juicy **apples**, cut in half

5 **carrots**, unpeeled

2 in **fresh ginger**, peeled

abc – apple, beets, and carrot – keeps the doc away!

1 Put all the ingredients in the juicer, adding the ginger in between the apple pieces while juicing.

2 Pour into glasses.

2½ cups **pineapple juice**

3 in **fresh ginger**, juiced

ice cubes

soda water

4 **pineapple slices**, to decorate

ginger beer – south India style

1 Pour the pineapple and ginger juices into a large tumbler with ice cubes and top up with soda.

2 Decorate with thinly sliced pineapple.

1 **fennel bulb**, roughly chopped

2 **cucumbers**, halved

6 **apples**, halved

cucumber swirls, to garnish

fennel, cucumber, and apple juice

1 Put all the ingredients in a juicer.

2 Make cucumber swirls using a vegetable peeler.

3 Pour into glasses and garnish with the cucumber swirls.

3 **figs**, halved, plus slices to garnish

3 **oranges**

2 handfuls **green grapes**

fig, orange, and grape juice

1 Put all the ingredients in the juicer.

2 Pour into glasses and garnish with fig slices.

2 tbsp **tarragon leaves**

1 **lime**, peeled

2 **oranges**, peeled

2 **fennel bulbs**, halved

tarragon, lime, and fennel juice

1 Put all the ingredients in the juicer, adding the tarragon in between the oranges and fennel.

2 Pour into glasses.

15 large **carrots**, peeled

6–8 tbsp **sweet condensed milk**

ice cubes

pinch of **freshly grated nutmeg**

pinch of **ground cinnamon**

Jamaican carrot juice

1 Juice the carrots.

2 Shake the carrot juice and condensed milk together with ice cubes in a shaker and strain into glasses.

3 Sprinkle with a pinch of the spices on top.

3–4 **lemons**

1 cup **elderflower cordial**

3 tbsp **sugar syrup**

soda or sparkling water

ice cubes

lemon / lime slices, to decorate

elderflower cooler

1 Juice the lemons.

2 Mix the elderflower, lemon juice, and sugar syrup in tall glasses, stir and top up with soda/sparkling water.

3 Serve with ice and lemon/lime slices.

6–7 tbsp **tamarind pulp**

8 tbsp **sugar syrup**

2 cups **water**

ice cubes

pinch of **salt**

lime slices, to decorate

ice cubes

tamarind cooler

1 Mix all the ingredients in a blender and blend till you have a smooth texture.

2 Pour into glasses and decorate with the lime slices.

4–5 **sweet apples** or 1 ½ cups apple juice from carton

ice cubes

1 ½ cups **cranberry juice**, from a carton

soda water

apple slices, to decorate

cranberry and apple schorle

1 Juice the apples if using fresh apple juice.

2 Put ice in glasses and pour the juices over.

3 Top up with soda water and decorate with apple slices.

pulp from 4 **passion fruits**

1 cup **passion fruit syrup**

ice cubes

soda water

passionate lemonade

1 Muddle passion fruit pulp together with half the syrup in each glass and add a few ice cubes.

2 Top up with soda water and float the rest of the syrup on top of the drink.

½ tbsp **rosemary leaves**

4 **apples**, halved

4 **pears**, halved

1 **lemon**, peeled, plus slices to decorate

rosemary, apple, and pear juice

1 Put all the ingredients in the juicer and add the rosemary in between the apples and pears.

2 Pour into 4 glasses and garnish with lemon slices.

2 cups **roiboos tea**, chilled

½ cup **sugar syrup**

1 handful **raspberries**, roughly chopped

ice cubes

1½ cups **soda water**

roiboos and raspberry cooler

1 Brew the tea and allow it to cool.

2 In a pitcher, add the strained tea, sugar syrup, and raspberries and let stand in the fridge for 30 minutes to infuse.

3 Pour into 4 glasses over ice cubes and top up with soda water.

2 handfuls **red currants**

3 tbsp **sugar**

½ cup **sugar syrup**

ice cubes

lemon slices, to decorate

2½ cups **soda water**

red currant cooler

1 Shake the red currants and sugar together in a bowl, leave to infuse for 20 minutes.

2 Mash the currants with a wooden spoon and add the sugar syrup.

3 Put the mixture into 4 glasses, add the ice cubes and lemon slices, and top up with soda.

shakes

1 large **papaya**

2 large **blood oranges**

½ cup **aloe vera juice**

ice cubes

aloe vera and papaya shake

1 Cut 4 small slices from the papaya for decoration and set them aside. Peel the rest of the papaya, remove the seeds and roughly chop the flesh. Place the flesh in a blender, blend until smooth then pass though a fine sieve.

2 Cut the oranges in half and cut a slice from one of them. Cut this slice into quarters to use as decoration and set aside. Squeeze the juice from the remaining oranges and sieve to remove the seeds.

3 Mix together the papaya, orange, and aloe vera juices. Fill 4 glasses with ice, pour in the juice and decorate with the reserved papaya and orange slices.

3 cups **milk**

2 **bananas**, roughly chopped

4 tsp **sugar**

2 tbsp **poppy seeds**

7 oz **raspberries**

blueberry and poppy seed shake

1 Place the milk, bananas, and 2 teaspoons of the sugar in a blender and blend until smooth.

2 Place the poppy seeds on a saucer. Dip the rims of 4 glasses into the milkshake mixture and then into the poppy seeds.

3 Mash the raspberries and the remaining sugar with a fork and carefully spoon into the bottom of each of the glasses.

4 Blend the shake mixture again with the remaining poppy seeds, pour it over the raspberries and serve.

small bunch **parsley**, chopped

small bunch **cilantro**, chopped

2 sprigs **mint**, chopped

12 **basil leaves**, chopped

1 large **cucumber**, peeled, seeds removed, and flesh roughly chopped

2 cups **plain yogurt**

juice of 1 **lime**

4 **ice cubes**

1 handful **alfalfa sprouts**

herb and sprouts shake

1 Set aside a little of each of the chopped herbs for the garnish.

2 Put the remaining herbs in a blender with the cucumber, yogurt, lime juice, and ice. Blend until smooth then season with salt and pepper, pour into glasses and serve garnished with the reserved herbs and the alfalfa sprouts.

4½ oz **plain tofu**, drained and chopped

2 cups **plain yogurt**

1 cup **soy milk**

9 oz **raspberries**, plus extra to decorate

9 oz **blueberries**

1 **banana**

2 tbsp **honey**

berry tofu shake

1 Place the chopped tofu, yogurt, soy milk, berries, banana, and honey in a blender and blend until smooth.

2 Pour into glasses and serve with a few raspberries on top.

8 large **carrots**, peeled

2 in **fresh ginger**, peeled

2 cups **orange juice**

4 tbsp **plain yogurt**

chives, to garnish

carrot shake

1 Using a vegetable peeler, peel thin strips from half of one of the carrots, cut them into thin batons and set aside for the garnish.

2 Pass the remaining carrots and the ginger through a vegetable juicer. Mix the juice with the orange juice and yogurt and stir well.

3 Pour into glasses and garnish with the carrot strips and the chives.

2 cups **pineapple juice**
18 oz **raspberries**
2 cups **plain yogurt**
mint sprigs, to decorate

raspberry and pineapple shake

1 Place the pineapple juice, raspberries, and yogurt in a blender and blend until smooth.

2 Pour into glasses, decorate with the mint sprigs and serve.

6 tbsp **prepared boba/tapioca seeds**

½ cup **chamomile tea**

1 cup **black tea**, ceylon or assam

½ cup **milk**

5–6 tbsp **sugar syrup**

ice cubes

chamomile bubble tea

1 Boil the boba/tapica seeds according to the packet instructions. Rinse with plenty of cold water and drain before use.

2 Meanwhile, brew the chamomile and black tea, then chill for 20–30 minutes.

3 Pour the strained teas into a cocktail shaker together with the milk, sugar syrup, and ice cubes.

4 Strain into glasses and add the seeds. Serve with extra-wide straws to get some seeds with each sip.

2 cups **Guinness stout**

½ cup **sweet condensed milk**

½ tbsp **cocoa powder**

1 tsp **vanilla essence**

6 drops **angostura bitters**

pinch of **freshly grated nutmeg**

ice cubes

1 tbsp chopped **salty peanuts**, to garnish

Guinness punch

1 Mix all the ingredients in a blender and blend till you have a smooth texture.

2 Pour into glasses and garnish with the chopped peanuts.

4 **oranges**

2 **bananas**

4 scoops **vanilla ice cream**

2 cups **milk**

creamy orange shake

1 Cut 4 strips of peel from one of the oranges, twist into spirals and set aside for the decoration.

2 Squeeze the juice from the oranges and place in a blender with the remaining ingredients.

3 Blend until smooth then pour into glasses and decorate with the twists of orange peel.

MAKES 4 servings   **PREP TIME** 1 hr   **DIFFICULTY** easy

½ oz **dried seaweed**

1 cup **warm water**

1 large **cucumber**

½ cup **aloe vera juice**

2 tbsp **chopped mint**, plus sprigs to garnish

ice cubes

cucumber, seaweed, and aloe vera shake

1 Place the seaweed in a bowl with the water and set aside to soak for 45 minutes.

2 Cut 12 thin slices from the cucumber and set aside for the garnish. Roughly chop the rest of the cucumber.

3 Place the chopped cucumber in a blender with the soaked seaweed and its liquor, the aloe vera juice, and the chopped mint.

4 Blend until smooth then strain through a fine sieve. Pour the juice into glasses filled with ice and garnish with the cucumber slices and the mint sprigs.

MAKES 4 servings   **PREP TIME** 10 min   **DIFFICULTY** easy

9 oz **blueberries**

9 oz **red currants**

1 cup **plain yogurt**

2 cups **milk**

2 tbsp **honey**

blueberry shake

1 Set aside a small handful of the blueberries and red currants and place the rest in a blender with the yogurt, milk, and honey.

2 Blend until smooth then pour into 4 glasses.

3 Drop the reserved blueberries and red currants into the glasses and serve the shakes immediately.

2 **mangoes**

3 cups **milk**

2 scoops **vanilla ice cream**

juice of 1 **lime**

2 tbsp **honey**

mint sprigs, to decorate

mango milkshake

1 Cut 8 small slices from the end of one of the mangoes and set them aside for the decoration.

2 Peel the remaining mangoes and remove the pits. Roughly chop the flesh and place in a blender with the milk, ice cream, lime juice, and honey.

3 Blend until smooth then pour into glasses and serve decorated with the reserved mango slices and the mint sprigs.

9 oz **raspberries**

3 cups **buttermilk**

4 **ice cubes**

2 tbsp **honey**

mint sprigs, to decorate

raspberry buttermilk shake

1 Set aside 12 raspberries for the decoration. Place the rest of the raspberries in a blender with the buttermilk, ice cubes, and honey and blend until smooth.

2 Pour into 4 glasses and serve decorated with the reserved raspberries and the mint.

6 tbsp **raspberry milkshake syrup**

4 tbsp **sugar**

2 **egg whites**, lightly whisked

3 cups **milk**

seeds from 2 **vanilla pods**

1 cup **cream**

marshmallows, threaded onto wooden skewers, to serve

raw egg
see page 4

vanilla shake

1 Mix about 2 teaspoons of the raspberry syrup with the sugar to stain some of the crystals and spread the mixture on a plate. Set aside to dry for 15 minutes.

2 Once dry, using a pastry brush, paint vertical stripes of egg white on the outside of 4 glasses and roll them in the colored sugar to coat the egg white. Carefully brush off any excess sugar and set aside for 15 minutes.

3 Pour the remaining raspberry syrup into the bottom of the glasses. Put the remaining egg white in a blender with the milk, vanilla seeds, and cream and blend until smooth.

4 Pour the mixture into the glasses and serve immediately with the marshmallows alongside.

1 **vanilla pod**

4 cups **soft-serve chocolate chip ice cream**

½ cup **strong black coffee**, cold

4 scoops **chocolate ice cream**

1 tsp **ground cinnamon**

3 cups **milk**

Christmas mocha shake

1 Cut the vanilla pod lengthways into 4 pieces.

2 Spoon the chocolate chip ice cream into a piping bag fitted with a large star nozzle and set it aside to soften a little while you make the shakes.

3 Put the coffee, chocolate ice cream, cinnamon, and milk in a blender and blend until smooth. Quickly pour into 4 chilled glasses and pipe a swirl of chocolate chip ice cream on the top of each.

4 Garnish with the vanilla pods and serve immediately.

6 large scoops **chocolate ice cream**

2 **bananas**

3 tbsp **hazelnut syrup** (or other nut-flavored syrup)

ice cubes

2 tbsp chopped and toasted **hazelnuts**, to decorate

chocolate and banana shake with hazelnuts

1 Mix all the ingredients in a blender and blend till you have a smooth texture.

2 Pour into 4 glasses and garnish with the chopped hazelnuts.

1½ handfuls chopped **rhubarb**, fresh or frozen
2 handfuls **strawberries**
1½ cups **milk**
3 scoops **vanilla ice cream**
2 tsp **vanilla sugar**

rhubarb and strawberry milkshake

1 Mix all the ingredients in a blender and blend till you have a smooth texture.

2 Pour into 4 tall glasses with straws.

2 cups **milk**

1 cup **cream**

½ cup **strong black coffee**
sweetened with 4 tbsp sugar, cold

1 **egg white**

4 small scoops **vanilla ice cream**

1 oz **dark chocolate**, grated

coffee shake

1 Place the milk and cream in a blender with the coffee and egg white.

2 Blend until smooth and frothy then pour into 4 glasses. Place the ice cream on the top of the shakes, scatter over the grated chocolate and serve immediately.

raw egg
see page 4

9 oz **strawberries**, hulled and roughly chopped,
plus 4 whole fruits to decorate

juice of 4 **grapefruit**

ice cubes

strawberry and grapefruit shake

1 Place the chopped strawberries in a blender with the grapefruit juice.

2 Blend until smooth then pour into glasses filled with ice and garnish with the whole strawberries.

12 oz **crunchy peanut butter**

3 cups **milk**

4 scoops **vanilla ice cream**

peanut butter shake

1 Place all the ingredients in a blender and blend until smooth.

2 Pour into 4 glasses and serve immediately.

MAKES 4 servings   **PREP TIME** 10 min   **DIFFICULTY** easy

4 ripe **peaches**

2 cups **plain yogurt**

2 tbsp **honey**

1 tbsp **lemon juice**

8 **ice cubes**

peach yogurt shake

1 Cut one of the peaches into wedges and set aside.

2 Peel the remaining peaches, discard the pits and roughly chop the flesh.

3 Put the chopped peach flesh in a blender with the remaining ingredients and blend until smooth. Pour into glasses, add the peach wedges and serve.

4 scoops **chocolate chip ice cream**

2 **bananas**

3 cups **milk**

chocolate banana shake

1 Place all the ingredients in a blender and blend until smooth.

2 Pour into 4 glasses and serve immediately.

12 oz **frozen raspberries**

2 cups **plain yogurt**

2 **bananas**

4 tbsp **vanilla ice cream**

8 **fresh raspberries**, to decorate

mint sprigs, to decorate

raspberry shake

1 Place the frozen raspberries, yogurt, and bananas in a blender and blend until smooth.

2 Pour into glasses, top with the ice cream, and decorate with the fresh raspberries and sprigs of mint.

1 cup good **coffee**, chilled

4 scoops **chocolate ice cream**

½ tsp **ground cinnamon**

½ cup **milk**

ice cubes

mocha shake with cinnamon

1 Mix all the ingredients in a blender and blend till you have a smooth texture.

2 Pour into tall glasses and serve with straws.

1½ cups canned **mango pulp**

2 cups **buttermilk**

4 **green cardamom pods**, crushed

ice cubes

mango and cardamom lassi

1 Put all the ingredients in a cocktail shaker and shake well.

2 Strain the mixture into 4 glasses.

3 cups **milk**

4 tbsp **powdered drinking chocolate**, plus extra to decorate

1 tsp **ground cinnamon**

7 tbsp **cream**

chocolate shake

1 Blend 18 fl oz of the milk with 3 tablespoons of the chocolate powder and the cinnamon in a blender and pour into 4 glasses.

2 Blend the remaining milk and chocolate powder with half the cream and carefully pour into the glasses.

3 Lightly whip the remaining cream and spoon on top of the shakes. Sprinkle with chocolate powder and serve.

12 oz **cherries**, pits removed

2 cups **milk**

2 scoops **vanilla ice cream**

1¾ oz **dark chocolate**, grated

cherry and chocolate shake

1 Place the cherries in a blender with the milk and ice cream and blend until smooth.

2 Pour into glasses and sprinkle over the grated chocolate. Serve immediately.

9 oz **rhubarb**, roughly chopped

4 tbsp **brown sugar**

2 cups **almond milk**

1 stick **rhubarb**, sliced lengthways, to decorate

rhubarb and almond lassi

1 Place the rhubarb and sugar in a small pan with a splash of water. Cook gently for 10 minutes, taking care the rhubarb doesn't burn, then remove from the heat and set aside to cool.

2 Set aside 4 teaspoons of the cooled rhubarb then place the remainder in a blender. Add the almond milk and blend until smooth.

3 Pour into 4 glasses, spoon the reserved rhubarb on top and serve with the sliced rhubarb alongside.

9 oz **morello cherries** in syrup

2 cups **buttermilk**

morello cherry buttermilk smoothie

1 Blend the cherries and syrup with the buttermilk until smooth. Serve immediately.

MAKES 4 servings   PREP TIME 10 min   DIFFICULTY easy

4 tbsp **shredded coconut**

1⅔ cups **coconut milk**

juice from 4 **oranges**

8 **ice cubes**

sugar

orange zest, to decorate

naranja colada

1 Place the shredded coconut on a small plate. Moisten the rims of the serving glasses with a little water and dip into the coconut.

2 Place the coconut milk, orange juice, and ice cubes in a blender, blend thoroughly then sweeten to taste with a little sugar.

3 Pour into the glasses and sprinkle with the orange zest.

1⅔ cups **coconut milk**

1 cup **plain yogurt**

1 cup **pineapple juice**

sugar

fresh coconut, to decorate (optional)

pineapple and coconut shake

1 Blend the coconut milk with the yogurt and pineapple juice.

2 Sweeten to taste with the sugar, pour into glasses and serve decorated with a little fresh coconut, if you like.

*

4 **large carrots**, peeled, or 1 ½ cups carrot juice

1 cup **plain yogurt**

juice of 1 **lemon**

pinch **chili flakes**

4 **baby carrots**, to garnish

carrot shake

1 Juice the carrots.

2 Blend the carrot juice with the yogurt and lemon juice. Season with a little salt.

3 Pour into glasses, sprinkle with chili flakes and garnish with the baby carrots.

 **MAKES** 4 servings   **PREP TIME** 5 min   **DIFFICULTY** easy

2 large **avocadoes**, peeled and pits removed

½ cup **sweet condensed milk**

½ cup **apple or pear juice**

½ cup **milk**

ice cubes

✳ sweet avocado shake

1 Mix all the ingredients in a blender and blend till you have a smooth texture.

2 Pour into glasses.

6 scoops **chocolate ice cream**

3 tbsp **cocoa powder**, dissolved in hot water

pinch of **chili powder**

pinch of **ground cinnamon**

⅓ cup **cold coffee**

ice cubes

chocolate and chili shake

1 Mix all the ingredients in a blender and blend till you have a smooth texture.

2 Pour into glasses.

＊

1 cup **sea buckthorn purée**

1 cup **orange juice**

2 cups **buttermilk**

2 **lady fingers**, broken into pieces

orange zest, to decorate

mint sprigs, to decorate

orange and sea buckthorn shake

1 Put the buckthorn purée, orange juice, and buttermilk together in a blender.

2 Blend together to combine and pour into 4 glasses.

3 Top each with a piece of lady finger, a sprinkle of orange zest, and a sprig of mint to serve.

2 **ripe pears**, peeled, quartered, cored, and chopped

3 cups **plain yogurt**

2 tbsp **honey**

½ tsp **ground cinnamon**, plus extra to decorate

pinch of **grated nutmeg**

spiced pear and yogurt shake

1 Put the pear, yogurt, honey, cinnamon, and nutmeg into a blender and blend until smooth.

2 Pour into glasses and sprinkle each with a little cinnamon to serve.

4 **bananas**, sliced

1 cup **plain yogurt**

1 cup **walnuts**, chopped, plus 2 tsp extra to decorate

2 tbsp **honey**

banana and walnut shake

1 Put the bananas into a blender and add the yogurt, walnuts, and honey.

2 Blend until thoroughly blended, pour into glasses and sprinkle with the extra chopped walnuts.

14 oz **strawberries**, halved

⅞ cup **plain yogurt**

1 ⅓ cups **milk**

dash **lemon juice**

2 tbsp **honey**

strawberry shake

1 Put all the ingredients into a blender and blend until smooth.

2 Pour into chilled glasses. Add ice cubes if you wish.

✳

6 **kiwi fruit**, peeled

10 tsp **aloe vera juice**

⅞ cup **plain yogurt**

⅞ cup **apple juice**

mint sprigs, to decorate

kiwi fruit and aloe vera shake

1 Place the kiwi fruit, aloe vera juice, yogurt, and apple juice in a blender and blend until smooth.

2 Strain through a fine sieve and serve over ice decorated with the mint sprigs.

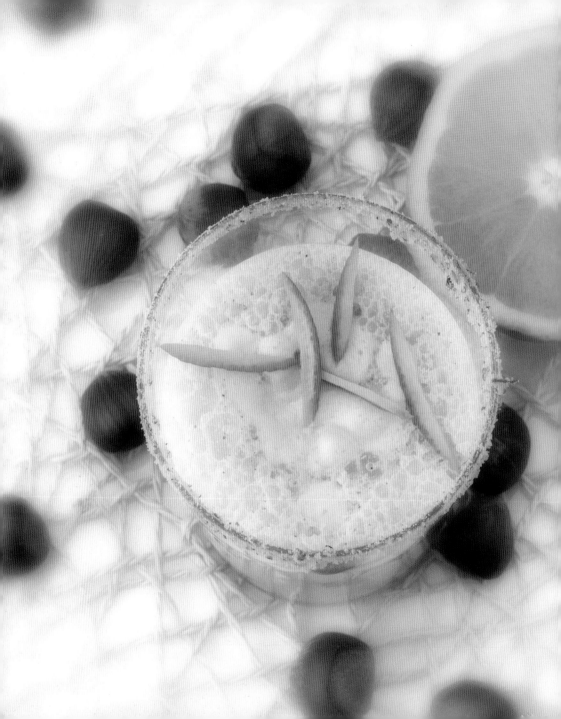

1 **orange**

1¼ cups **hazelnuts**, finely chopped

3 cups **milk**

4 scoops **vanilla ice cream**

hazelnut milkshake

1 Slice the orange in half and remove the peel from one half. Cut the peel into strips and set aside for the decoration. Juice the 2 orange halves.

2 Place a little of the juice in a saucer and dip the rims of 4 glasses into the juice. Dip the moistened rims into the hazelnuts and set aside.

3 Place the remaining hazelnuts in a blender with the milk and orange juice. Blend until smooth then carefully pour into the glasses.

4 Place a scoop of ice cream in each glass and decorate with the reserved orange peel.

½ cup **toffee or caramel sauce**

½ cup **apple sauce**

3 scoops **banana ice cream**

½ cup **milk**

ice cubes

toffee apple and banana shake

1 Mix all the ingredients in a blender and blend till you have a smooth texture.

2 Pour into 4 glasses.

6 scoops **chocolate ice cream**

4 tbsp **peanut butter**

1 cup **milk**

chocolate flakes, to decorate

chopped peanuts, to decorate

peanut butter and chocolate shake

1 Mix the ice cream, peanut butter, and milk in a blender and blend until you have a smooth texture.

2 Pour into glasses and sprinkle over the peanuts and chocolate flakes.

3 large ripe **pears**

3 cups **milk**

6 tbsp **aloe vera juice**

2 tbsp **honey**

ice cubes

pear and aloe vera shake

1 Cut the pears in half, remove the cores and carefully cut 4 thin slices for the decoration.

2 Peel the rest of the pears and roughly chop the flesh. Place the pears in a blender with the milk, aloe vera juice, and honey.

3 Blend until smooth then pour into glasses over ice and decorate with the pear slices.

4 **white-fleshed nectarines**, peeled, pits removed, and roughly chopped

3 cups **plain yogurt**

2 tbsp **honey**

cookies, to serve

nectarine yogurt shake

1 Place the nectarines, yogurt, and honey in a blender and blend until smooth.

2 Pour into glasses and serve with your favorite cookies.

3 cups **milk**

2 scoops **vanilla ice cream**

1 **banana**, roughly chopped

½ tsp **vanilla essence**

½ cup **blue syrup** or 5 drops blue coloring

sugar, to taste

mint sprigs, to decorate

mint milkshake

1 Put the milk, ice cream, banana, vanilla essence, and syrup or food coloring in a blender and blend until smooth. Add sugar to taste then blend once more.

2 Pour into glasses and serve with the mint sprigs.

⅞ cup **pineapple juice**

⅞ cup **coconut cream**

2 scoops **vanilla ice cream**

pineapple wedges

4 straws

4 cocktail umbrellas

✳ guilt-free chi chi

1 Place the pineapple juice, coconut cream, and ice cream in a blender and blend until smooth.

2 Pour into glasses and serve immediately decorated with the pineapple wedges, straws, and umbrellas.

4 large **bananas**

4 cups **milk**

4 tsp **honey**

¼ tsp **grated nutmeg**

ground cinnamon, to decorate

spiced banana flip

1 Peel the bananas and cut into chunks.

2 Put into a blender or food processor with the remaining ingredients and blend until smooth.

3 Pour into chilled glasses and sprinkle with ground cinnamon.

7 oz **strawberries**

4 tbsp **sugar**

juice of 1 **lemon**

2 cups **milk**

2 **bananas**

4 tbsp **strawberry flavored syrup**

strawberry swirl

1 Set aside 4 of the strawberries for decoration.

2 Take two-thirds of the remaining strawberries and mash them with the sugar and lemon juice. Press the mixture through a fine sieve and divide between 4 glasses.

3 Put the remaining strawberries in a blender with the milk and bananas and blend until smooth.

4 Pour into the glasses and drizzle a little of the syrup around the rim of the glasses. Decorate with the reserved strawberries and serve.

2 tbsp **sugar**
½ cup **strong black coffee**
2 cups **milk**
1 cup **cream**
ice cubes
1 oz **dark chocolate**, finely grated

iced coffee with cream

1 Dissolve the sugar in the coffee and let it cool.

2 Mix the coffee with the milk and half the cream and pour into glasses over ice.

3 Whip the remaining cream, put it in a piping bag fitted with a small nozzle and pipe on top of the coffee.

4 Sprinkle over the grated chocolate and serve immediately.

1 cup **orange juice**

6 scoops **chocolate ice cream**

1 tbsp **orange jam**

ice cubes

candied orange strips, to decorate

8 tbsp **whipped cream**, to decorate

chocolate and orange shake

1 Mix all the ingredients in a blender and blend till you have a smooth texture.

2 Pour into glasses and decorate with candied orange and whipped cream.

1 cup **orange juice**

6 scoops **vanilla ice cream**

1 tbsp **orange jam**

2 tsp **vanilla essence**

ice cubes

orange and vanilla shake

1 Mix all the ingredients in a blender and blend till you have a smooth texture.

2 Pour into 4 glasses.

4½ oz **raspberries**, plus extra to decorate

3 cups **milk**

2 scoops **raspberry ripple ice cream**

✳ raspberry milkshake

1 Place the raspberries, milk, and ice cream in a blender and blend until smooth.

2 Pour into glasses, decorate with the raspberries and serve immediately.

1 **banana**

3 cups **milk**

juice of 2 **limes**

2 scoops **vanilla ice cream**

3 drops **blue food coloring**

lime spider with ice cream

1 Cut 4 slices from the banana and set aside.

2 Place the remaining banana in a blender with the milk, lime juice, ice cream, and blue coloring. Blend until smooth then pour into glasses and serve with the reserved banana slices on top.

2 **assam tea bags**

3 cups **milk**

1 **cinnamon stick**, crushed, plus 4 to decorate

½ tsp **ground nutmeg**

½ tsp **ground ginger**

6 **cloves**

1 tsp **vanilla extract**

3 tbsp **honey**

⅔ cup **cream**, lightly whipped

ground mixed spice, to decorate

✳ Christmas chai grog

1 Put the tea bags in a pan with the milk, crushed cinnamon stick, nutmeg, ginger, cloves, vanilla extract, and honey.

2 Heat gently until boiling then reduce the heat and simmer for 5 minutes. Remove the pan from the heat, remove and discard the tea bags and let the mixture steep for 10 minutes.

3 Strain the grog through a fine sieve, return to the pan and gently re-heat then pour into glasses and top with the whipped cream. Sprinkle with the mixed spice and add a cinnamon stick to each.

12 **kiwi fruit**

2 **bananas**

2 cups **apple juice**

4 **mint sprigs**, to decorate

4 **raspberries**, to decorate

kiwi fruit and banana shake

1 Cut 8 thin slices from one of the kiwi fruits and set aside. Peel the remaining kiwis, roughly chop the flesh and place in a blender.

2 Cut 4 slices from one of the bananas and set aside. Roughly chop the remaining bananas and place in the blender.

3 Add the apple juice, blend until smooth and pour into 4 glasses. Thread the reserved kiwi and banana slices onto cocktail sticks with the mint sprigs and raspberries and place on top of the glasses.

8 tbsp **dark cocoa powder** dissolved in hot water

2½ cups **milk**

4 tbsp **mint syrup**

ice cubes

8 **mint leaves**, to decorate

chocolate and mint shake

1 Mix all the ingredients in a blender and blend till you have a smooth texture.

2 Pour into glasses and decorate with fresh mint leaves.

5 tbsp small **sago pearls**, cooked and chilled

6 tbsp **vermicelli** (soak in warm water for 5–10 min)

ice cubes

2 tbsp **rose syrup**

2 cups **milk**

4 tbsp **vanilla ice cream**

1 tbsp finely chopped **pistachios** or cashews, to decorate

falooda

1 Simmer the sago pearls in enough water to cover them over low heat for 25–30 minutes. Cook till they are tender but still chewy. Sago pearls can be stored in fridge for later use, just drain them and cover them with water in airtight container.

2 Put the noodles, sago pearls, and ice cubes into tall glasses.

3 Pour in the syrup and milk and decorate with ice cream and nuts.

4 Serve with a spoon.

2 cups **vanilla soy milk**

2 tbsp **tahini paste**

1 tbsp **sesame seeds**, unpolished

2 tbsp **honey**

½ tbsp **wasabi powder**, dissolved in a bit of water

ice cubes

wasabi and sesame shake

1 Mix all the ingredients in a blender and blend till you have a smooth texture.

2 Pour into 4 glasses.

3 scoops **vanilla ice cream**

3 handfuls **blueberries**

1½ cups **coconut milk**

toasted coconut flakes, to decorate

coconut and blueberry shake

1 Mix all the ingredients in a blender and blend till you have a smooth texture.

2 Pour into 4 glasses and decorate with coconut flakes.

4 scoops **vanilla ice cream**

10 large **carrots**, peeled

Iranian carrot juice float

1 Juice the carrots.

2 Pour carrot juice into 4 sundae glasses.

3 Float a scoop of vanilla ice cream on top of each drink.

4 **bananas**, chopped

1 ½ tsp **vanilla extract** or vanilla sugar

½ cups **maple syrup**, plus 4 tsp to serve

2 cups **milk**

ice cubes

banana and maple milk shake

1 Put all the ingredients in a blender and blend till you have a smooth texture.

2 Pour into 4 glasses and top with a teaspoon of maple syrup in each glass.

2 tbsp **basil seeds** (tukmaria), soaked in cold water for 10–15 min

3 tbsp **rose water**

4 tbsp **sugar syrup**

1 tbsp **unsalted pistachios**, finely chopped

2½ cups **milk**

ice cubes

vishnu in the sea of milk

1 Pour all the ingredients into a large pitcher and stir to combine.

2 Pour into tall glasses and serve with a spoon.

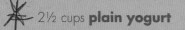

2½ cups **plain yogurt**

10 **dates**, pitted and chopped

3 **bananas**, chopped

ice cubes

banana and date smoothie

1 Mix all the ingredients in a blender and blend till you have a smooth texture.

2 Pour into 4 glasses.

3 **bananas**, chopped

3 handfuls **blackberries**

2½ cups **milk**

sugar to taste (optional)

ice cubes

blackberry and banana shake

1 Place all the ingredients in a blender and blend till you have a smooth texture.

2 Pour into 4 glasses.

6 **oreo cookies**, crushed

8 scoops **vanilla ice cream**

1 cup **milk**

2 handfuls **raspberries**, reserve a few to decorate

oreo and raspberry shake

1 Mix all the ingredients in a blender and blend till you have a smooth texture.

2 Pour into 4 glasses and decorate with extra raspberries.

2 tbsp **roasted pecan nuts**, plus 2 tbsp extra, chopped, to decorate

5 tbsp **toffee sauce**

8 scoops **vanilla ice cream**

1 cup **milk**

1 tsp **vanilla essence**

1 **banana**

pecan and vanilla shake

1 Mix all the ingredients in a blender and blend till you have a smooth texture.

2 Pour into 4 glasses and scatter over some chopped pecan nuts.

3 handfuls **raspberries**

4 scoops **vanilla ice cream**

ice cubes

1 tsp **liquorice powder**

raspberry and liquorice shake

1 Put the raspberries, ice cream, and ice cubes in a blender and blend till you have a smooth texture.

2 Pour into 4 glasses and sprinkle the liquorice powder on top.

4 strong **espressos**

1½ cups **cold water**

½ cup **sweet condensed milk**

1 tsp **cardamom powder**

ice cubes

Vietnamese iced coffee

1 Brew the espressos and mix with the cold water.

2 Put ice cubes in 4 glasses and pour over the condensed milk.

3 Sprinkle with cardamom and top off with coffee.

4 Add more condensed milk if you prefer your coffee sweeter or creamier.

5–6 scoops **dark chocolate ice cream**

2 handfuls **cherries**, pitted

3 tbsp **cherry schnapps / liqueur**

1 cup **milk**

ice cubes (optional)

pinch of **grated chocolate**, to decorate

chocolate and cherry shake

1 Mix all the ingredients in a blender and blend till you have a smooth texture.

2 Pour into 4 glasses and add ice, if you like. Serve sprinkled with grated chocolate.

smoothies

18 oz **blackcurrants**

1¾ oz **sugar**

½ cup **water**

2 cups **plain yogurt**

juice of 1 **lemon**

blackcurrant smoothie

1 Place the blackcurrants in a small pan with the sugar and water. Heat gently until the sugar has dissolved and the fruit is soft then transfer to a bowl and let cool for 1 hour.

2 Put the blackcurrants in a blender with the remaining ingredients, blend until smooth then pour into glasses and serve.

1⅔ cups **condensed milk**

juice and zest of 4 **limes**

4 tbsp **honey**

2 handfuls **ice cubes**

lime slices and leaves, to decorate

key lime pie smoothie

1 Place the condensed milk, lime juice and zest, honey, and ice cubes in a blender and blend until smooth.

2 Spoon into glasses and serve decorated with the lime slices and leaves.

1 large **papaya**, peeled and seeds removed

2 **limes**

2 cups **coconut water**

1 cup **cold water**

papaya and coconut drink

1 Cut small slices from the papaya and set aside. Roughly chop the remaining flesh.

2 Cut 4 small slices from the limes and set aside. Juice the remaining limes.

3 Place the chopped papaya in a blender with the lime juice, coconut water, and water and blend until smooth.

4 Pour into chilled glasses and serve decorated with the papaya and lime slices.

MAKES 4 servings   PREP TIME 10 min   DIFFICULTY easy

8 **kiwi fruit**, peeled
2 in **fresh ginger**, peeled and grated
juice of 2 **limes**
juice of 2 **oranges**
lime slices, to decorate
orange slices, to decorate
lemongrass, to decorate

kiwi fruit and ginger smoothie

1 Roughly chop the kiwi fruit and place in a blender with the ginger, lime juice, and orange juice.

2 Blend until smooth, pour into glasses and decorate with the lime and orange slices and the lemongrass.

½ small **watermelon**, peeled, seeds removed, flesh roughly chopped

2 cups **plain yogurt**

juice of 1 **lime**

8 **ice cubes**

4 sprigs **mint**, to decorate

watermelon smoothie

1 Place the watermelon in a blender with the yogurt, lime juice, and ice.

2 Blend until smooth then pour into 4 glasses and serve decorated with the mint sprigs.

MAKES 4 servings   **PREP TIME** 10 min   **DIFFICULTY** easy

9 oz **blackberries**

9 oz **raspberries**

9 oz **blueberries**

2 cups **apple juice**

1 cup **plain yogurt**

mint sprigs, to decorate

forest fruits smoothie

1 Place the berries in a blender with the apple juice and yogurt and blend until smooth.

2 Pour into glasses and serve decorated with the mint sprigs.

4 **bananas**

2 cups **apple juice**

1 cup **pineapple juice**

juice of 1 **lime**

banana juice

1 Place the ingredients in a blender and blend until smooth.
Serve immediately.

6 **red apples**

4 tbsp **honey**

2 cups **plain yogurt**

1 tsp **ground cinnamon**

4 scoops **vanilla ice cream**

baked apple smoothie

1 Heat the oven to 230°F. Cut one of the apples in half horizontally and cut 8 very thin slices. Place these on a rack and bake in the oven for 30 minutes or until the apple slices are golden brown.

2 Turn the oven up to 350°F. Remove the cores from the rest of the apples, keeping them whole, and place the apples on a baking tray. Bake for 30 minutes or until they are very soft then remove from the oven and let them cool for 15 minutes.

3 Remove the skins from the apples and place the flesh in a blender with the honey, yogurt, and cinnamon. Blend until smooth then pour into glasses and add the ice cream. Decorate with the dried apple slices and serve immediately.

1 small **papaya**

2 **bananas**

3 cups **plain yogurt**

juice of 1 **lime**

4 **ice cubes**

papaya smoothie

1 Cut 4 small slices from the end of the papaya and set aside.

2 Peel the rest of the papaya and remove the seeds. Place the flesh in a blender with the remaining ingredients and blend until smooth.

3 Pour into glasses, decorate with the papaya slices and serve immediately.

3 **bananas**

2 handfuls **strawberries**

1 cup **coconut milk**

4 tbsp **shredded coconut**

1 cup **plain yogurt**

ice cubes

banana, strawberry, and coconut smoothie

1 Mix all the ingredients in a blender and blend till you have a smooth texture.

2 Pour into 4 glasses.

4 **limes**, peeled

6 tbsp **sugar syrup**

1 handful **mint leaves**

2 cups **water**

ice cubes

minty lemonade

1 Mix the limes, sugar syrup, and mint in a blender and blend for 1 minute.

2 Add the water and blend for 1–2 minutes.

3 Pour over ice into 4 glasses.

3 cups **plain yogurt**

2 **bananas**

5 oz **smooth peanut butter**

2 scoops **vanilla ice cream**

peanut butter smoothie

1 Place all the ingredients in a blender and blend until smooth.

2 Pour into 4 glasses and serve immediately.

14 oz **tinned peaches** in juice

2 **bananas**, roughly chopped

1 cup **passion fruit juice**

1 cup **milk**

seeds and flesh from 2 **passion fruit**, to decorate

peach and passion fruit smoothie

1 Place the peaches, bananas, passion fruit juice, and milk in a blender and blend until smooth.

2 Pour into glasses and serve with the passion fruit seeds and flesh scattered over.

3 cups **coconut milk**

2 **bananas**

juice of 1 **lime**

2 tbsp **runny honey**

1 tsp **ground cinnamon**

coconut and banana smoothie

1 Place the coconut milk, bananas, and lime juice in a blender and blend until smooth.

2 Pour into glasses, drizzle over the honey and sprinkle with the cinnamon.

½ small **watermelon**, peeled and seeds removed

14 oz **strawberries**, hulled and roughly chopped

juice of 1 **lime**

18 oz **plain yogurt**

strawberry and watermelon smoothie

1 Roughly chop the watermelon flesh and place in a blender with the strawberries and lime juice.

2 Blend until smooth then pour into glasses and add the yogurt. Swirl with a straw or wooden stirrer and serve immediately.

9 oz **raspberries**

9 oz **cranberries**

1 cup **plain yogurt**

1 cup **cranberry juice**

juice of 1 **lime**

2 tbsp **honey**

12 **ice cubes**

cranberry and raspberry smoothie

1 Place all the ingredients in a blender and blend until smooth.

2 Pour into glasses and serve immediately.

3 **kiwi fruit**, peeled

2 **bananas**, peeled and roughly chopped

3 cups **milk**

kiwi fruit and banana smoothie

1 Cut 1 slice of kiwi fruit, cut it into quarters, and skewer each one with a cocktail stick. Set aside.

2 Place the remaining kiwi fruit, the bananas, and the milk in a blender and blend until smooth.

3 Serve with the kiwi fruit skewer balanced over the glass.

1 large **cucumber**, peeled

2 **avocados**, peeled, pits removed and roughly chopped

2 cups **plain yogurt**

juice of 2 **limes**

avocado and cucumber smoothie

1 Cut the cucumber in half lengthways and scrape out the seeds. Dice the flesh and set aside 8 pieces.

2 Place the remaining cucumber in a blender with the avocado, yogurt, and lime juice. Pour into glasses and serve decorated with the diced cucumber.

3 cups **pineapple juice**

9 oz **blueberries**

12 **ice cubes**

mint sprigs, to decorate

blueberry and pineapple smoothie

1 Place the pineapple juice, blueberries, and ice cubes in a blender and blend until slushy.

2 Pour into glasses and serve decorated with mint.

MAKES 4 servings   PREP TIME 10 min   DIFFICULTY easy

9 oz **raspberries**

3½ cups **coconut milk**

1 **banana**

2 tbsp **honey**

popcorn, to serve (optional)

raspberry and coconut smoothie

1 Set aside a few of the raspberries for decoration.

2 Place the remaining raspberries in a blender with the coconut milk, banana, and honey and blend until smooth.

3 Pour into glasses filled with ice and serve decorated with the reserved raspberries and the popcorn alongside, if you like.

2 cups **vanilla-flavored soy**

6 fresh **figs**, halved

15 **walnut kernels**

ice cubes

figs, walnut, and vanilla soy smoothie

1 Mix all the ingredients in a blender and blend till you have a smooth texture.

2 Pour into tall glasses with straws.

2 cups **coconut milk**

6 tbsp **palm sugar**

½ tsp **salt**

ice cubes

½ sweet **honeydew melon**, peeled and cut into small chunks

Thai melon and coconut smoothie

1 Simmer the coconut milk, sugar, and salt on low heat for 10 minutes. Chill in the fridge for 10 minutes.

2 Add the ice cubes and coconut milk to a blender and blend until you have a smooth texture.

3 Put the melon chunks in 4 glasses and pour the coconut mixture over.

4 Serve with a spoon.

4½ oz **blueberries**

4½ oz **red currants**

1 **banana**

2 cups **plain yogurt**

2 tbsp chopped **almonds**

blueberry and red currant smoothie

1 Place the blueberries, red currants, banana, and yogurt in a blender and blend until smooth.

2 Pour into glasses, sprinkle over the chopped almonds and serve immediately.

seeds from 4 **pomegranates**

4½ oz **blueberries**

3 cups **plain yogurt**

1 **banana**

juice of 1 **lime**

pomegranate smoothie

1 Place all the ingredients in a blender and blend until smooth.

2 Pour into 4 glasses and serve.

4 tbsp **instant coffee granules**

1⅔ cups **coconut milk**

1⅔ cups **milk**

2 **bananas**, roughly chopped

1 oz **dark chocolate**, finely grated

coffee and coconut smoothie

1 Put the coffee, coconut milk, milk, and bananas in a blender and blend until smooth.

2 Pour into 4 glasses, sprinkle over the grated chocolate and serve.

2 **red peppers**, seeds removed and roughly chopped

4 **ripe tomatoes**, skinned, seeds removed and chopped

1 tsp **tabasco**

1 tbsp **white wine vinegar**

4 tbsp **water**

crushed peppercorns, to garnish

sliced baguette, to serve

pepper and vegetable smoothie

1 Blend together the peppers, tomatoes, tabasco, vinegar, and water.

2 Pass through a fine sieve, season with salt and pour into glasses.

3 Garnish with the crushed peppercorns and serve with the slices of baguette.

5 oz **frozen peas**

1 cup **green tea**

1 cup **plain yogurt**

2 tsp **wasabi powder**

1 ⅓ cups **water**

¼ cup **rice vinegar**

¾ tsp **lecithin powder**

green tea and wasabi smoothie

1 Cook the peas in little water. Drain and rinse under cold running water.

2 Blend the green tea with the peas and yogurt until smooth then pass through a fine sieve and set aside.

3 Mix the wasabi powder with a little of the water and add the remaining water, rice vinegar, and lecithin powder. Blend with a stick blender and chill in the fridge for 20 minutes.

4 Pour the smoothie into glasses. Blend the wasabi foam again, lifting the blender to incorporate as much air as possible. Let the mixture settle for 1 minute then scoop out the foam onto the smoothies. Serve immediately.

16 oz **ripe tomatoes**, skinned, seeds removed and roughly chopped

4 **ice cubes**

2 tbsp **chopped parsley**

2 tbsp **chopped basil**

2 tbsp **chopped dill**, plus fronds to garnish

1 **red chili**, seeds removed and finely chopped, plus 1 finely sliced chili to garnish

4 tbsp **plain yogurt**, to garnish

spicy tomato and herb drink

1 Place the tomatoes, ice cubes, herbs, and chopped chili in a blender and blend until smooth. Season with salt and pepper.

2 Pour into glasses and garnish with the yogurt, sliced chili and dill fronds.

4 ripe **nectarines**

2 cups **plain yogurt**

sugar

ice cubes

nectarine wedges, to serve

nectarine yogurt lassi

1 Peel the nectarines, remove the pits and roughly chop the flesh.

2 Blend the chopped nectarines with the yogurt until smooth, sweeten to taste with sugar and pour into glasses filled with ice.

3 Serve with the nectarine wedges.

2 cups **soy yogurt**

9 oz **raspberries**

sugar

½ cup **soy milk**

granola, to serve (optional)

raspberry and soy smoothie

1 Blend half the yogurt with the raspberries, sweeten to taste with the sugar and pour into 4 glasses.

2 Blend the remaining yogurt with the soy milk and carefully pour into the glasses on top of the raspberry mix. Serve immediately, sprinkled with a little granola, if you like.

6 **kiwi fruit**, peeled and chopped

½ **honeydew melon**, peeled, seeds removed and chopped

2 **pears**, peeled, cored, and chopped

2 tbsp **lemon juice**

6 **ice cubes**

sugar, to taste

kiwi fruit, melon, and pear smoothie

1 Place the pieces of kiwi fruit, melon, and pear into a blender with the lemon juice and ice and blend until smooth.

2 Add sugar to taste and serve.

1 cup **coconut milk**

1 ½ cups **plain yogurt**

2 **bananas**

3 tbsp **sesame seeds**

ice cubes

coconut and banana smoothie

1 Mix all the ingredients in a blender and blend till you have a smooth texture.

2 Pour into 4 glasses.

2 tsp **matcha green tea powder**

4 tbsp **honey**

1½ cups **plain yogurt**

½ cups **apple juice**

3 tbsp **sesame seeds**

ice cubes

green tea smoothie

1 Mix all the ingredients in a blender and blend till you have a smooth texture.

2 Pour into 4 glasses.

3 If you prefer it sweeter, increase the amount of apple juice and reduce the amount of ice cubes.

9 oz **blueberries**

2 **bananas**

2 cups **plain yogurt**

blueberry smoothie

1 Put the blueberries, bananas, and yogurt into a blender and blend until smooth.

2 Pour into 4 glasses and serve.

2 **starfuit**, roughly chopped

2 **mangoes**, peeled, pits removed, and roughly chopped

4 **kiwi fruit**, peeled and roughly chopped

2 cups **pineapple juice**

1 **kiwi fruit**, sliced, to decorate

1 **starfruit**, sliced, to decorate

exotic fruit smoothie

1 Blend the chopped starfruit, mango, and kiwi fruit with the pineapple juice.

2 Pour into glasses and decorate with the sliced kiwis and starfruit.

5 cups **plain yogurt**

3 **bananas**

5 tsp **matcha green tea powder**

6 **ice cubes**

2 tbsp **honey**

matcha smoothie

1 Put all the ingredients in a blender and blend until smooth.

2 Serve.

4 **eggs**, separated
4 tbsp **honey**
3½ cups **milk**
4 tbsp **wheatgerm**
grated nutmeg, to taste
ground cinnamon, to taste

raw egg
see page 4

wheatgerm and egg smoothie

1 Mix the egg yolks and honey and beat with an electric whisk until pale and frothy.

2 Heat the milk until bubbles form at the edge of the pan. Do not allow the milk to boil.

3 In a separate bowl, whisk the egg whites until stiff.

4 Add the warm milk and wheatgerm to the egg yolk mixture and blend until smooth. Fold into the egg whites and add nutmeg and cinnamon to taste.

5 Pour into glasses and serve immediately.

2 cups **plain yogurt**

7 tbsp **milk**

2 **bananas**

3 cups **blueberries**, plus extra to decorate

8 **strawberries**, sliced

blueberry, strawberry, and banana smoothie

1 Put the yogurt, milk, bananas, and blueberries into a blender and blend until smooth.

2 Serve alongside a few blueberries and sliced strawberries.

2 cups **strawberries**

4½ oz **blueberries** (optional)

2 tbsp **ground almonds**

1 tbsp **almond syrup**

1 tbsp **strawberry syrup** (optional)

1⅓ cups **plain yogurt**

2 scoops **vanilla ice cream**

flaked almonds, to decorate

strawberry slices, to decorate

strawberry and almond smoothie

1 Place all the ingredients in a blender and blend until smooth.

2 Divide between 4 glasses and garnish with flaked almonds and strawberry slices.

3 **bananas**

3 cups **soy milk**

1 tbsp **honey**

4 stalks **rosemary**, to decorate

½ **cantaloupe melon**, to decorate

mint leaves, to decorate

soy and melon smoothie

1 Put the bananas and soy milk into a blender with the honey and blend until smooth.

2 Remove all but the top leaves from the rosemary stalks. Scoop balls from the melon and thread them onto the rosemary stalks.

3 Serve the smoothie with the melon skewers and some mint leaves.

1 **honeydew melon**

1 cup **plain yogurt**

juice of 1 **lime**

mint leaves, to decorate

chilled melon smoothie

1 Peel the melon and remove the seeds.

2 Put the melon flesh into a blender with the yogurt and lime juice and blend until smooth.

3 Chill for 1 hour and serve decorated with mint leaves.

3 **bananas**, sliced

2 cups **raspberries**, plus 8 extra to decorate

1 tbsp **honey**

2 ½ cups **pink grapefruit juice**

raspberry, banana, and pink grapefruit smoothie

1 Put the bananas, raspberries, honey, and grapefruit juice into a blender and blend until smooth.

2 Pour into 4 glasses and serve topped with a couple of raspberries on each.

1 small seedless **watermelon**, roughly chopped

1 **lime**, peeled

1 tbsp **mint leaves**, plus extra to decorate

2 tbsp **sugar syrup**

ice cubes

watermelon, lime, and mint smoothie

1 Mix all the ingredients in a blender and blend till you have a smooth texture.

2 Pour into 4 glasses.

1 handful **cherries**, pitted
2 handfuls **blueberries**
1½ cups **plain yogurt**
½ cup **cherry syrup**
ice cubes

cherry and blueberry smoothie

1 Mix all the ingredients in a blender and blend till you have a smooth texture.

2 Pour into 4 glasses.

4 **bananas**, cut into chunks

4 cups **milk**

4 tbsp **honey**

6 **ice cubes**, crushed

1 tsp **ground cinnamon**

1 tsp **ground cardamom**

banana smoothie with cinnamon and cardamom

1 Put the bananas, milk, honey, and ice into a blender and blend until smooth.

2 Pour into glasses and sprinkle with ground cinnamon and cardamom.

6 **kiwi fruit**, peeled and chopped

juice of 1 **lemon**

2 cups **pineapple juice**

1–2 tbsp **honey**

4 **ice cubes**

kiwi fruit and lemon smoothie

1 Place all the ingredients in a blender and blend until smooth.

2 Pour into glasses and serve immediately.

16 oz **mixed berries**, strawberries, blueberries, raspberries

2 cups **plain or strawberry yogurt**

7 tbsp **milk**

4 tsp clear **honey**

honey and berry smoothie

1 Put all the ingredients into a blender or food processor and blend until smooth.

2 Pour into chilled glasses.

1 **pineapple**, peeled
2 **carrots**, washed
1 **zucchini**, washed

carrot, zucchini, and pineapple juice

1 Quarter the pineapple and cut away the central woody core. Cut the flesh into long thin wedges.

2 Trim the end off the carrots and zucchini.

3 Pass the pineapple, carrots, and zucchini through a vegetable juicer and mix the juice well before serving.

1 ripe **mango**, flesh cut off the pit

1 **banana**, chopped

2 cups **plain yogurt**

3 tbsp **lemon juice**

1 tsp **ground cardamom**

2 tbsp **honey**

2 **ice cubes**

mango lassi

1 Place all the ingredients in a blender and blend until smooth.

2 Pour into glasses and serve.

12 large ripe **plums**
2 cups **plain yogurt**
2 tbsp **sugar**
6 **ice cubes**

plum smoothie

1 Peel 4 of the plums carefully and reserve the skins for the decoration.

2 Remove the pits from all the plums and place the flesh in a blender with the yogurt, sugar, and ice cubes.

3 Blend until smooth then pour into glasses and serve decorated with the reserved plum skins.

4 **apples**

⅞ cup **acai berry juice**

2 cups **plain yogurt**

2 tbsp **honey**

2 tbsp **brown sugar**

acai berry and apple smoothie

1 Peel and core 3 of the apples and place in a blender with the acai juice, yogurt, and honey.

2 Blend until smooth then pour into glasses.

3 Cut the remaining apple into chunks, removing the core and seeds, and dip into the brown sugar. Thread onto cocktail sticks and place on top of the glasses.

8 ripe **plums**, pits removed
4½ oz **raspberries**
4½ oz **blueberries**
2 cups **plain yogurt**

plum and berry smoothie

1 Place all the ingredients in a blender and blend until smooth.

2 Pour into 4 glasses and serve immediately.

2 large **mangoes**

2 cups **plain yogurt**

1 small bunch **mint**

mango and peppermint smoothie

1 Peel the mangoes and cut the flesh away from the pits. Reserve 4 slices of the mango for the decoration and place the rest in a blender with the yogurt.

2 Reserve 4 sprigs of mint and place the remaining leaves in the blender. Blend until smooth, pour into 4 glasses and decorate with the reserved mango and the mint sprigs.

1 tbsp **flaxseed**

1 tbsp **sunflower seed**

1 cups **mango pulp**

1 cups **coconut milk**

3 tbsp **honey**

ice cubes

mango, coconut, and flaxseed smoothie

1 Put the seeds in the blender and grind them for 1–2 minutes.

2 Now add the rest of the ingredients in the blender and blend till you have a smooth texture.

3 Pour into 4 glasses.

juice of 6 **tangerines**

2 **mangoes**, peeled and cubed

1¼ cups **plain yogurt**

2 tbsp **honey**

ice cubes

tangerine and mango smoothie

1 Mix all the ingredients in a blender and blend till you have a smooth texture.

2 Pour into 4 glasses.

1 large **cucumber**

2 cups **buttermilk**

dill sprigs, to garnish

cucumber buttermilk smoothie

1 Using a vegetable peeler, remove strips of the cucumber peel at even intervals. Cut 8 thin slices from the cucumber and set aside.

2 Cut the rest of the cucumber in half lengthways and remove the seeds. Cut the cucumber into chunks and place in a blender with the buttermilk. Blend until smooth then pour into 4 glasses.

3 Thread the cucumber slices onto cocktail sticks and place on top of the glasses. Garnish with the dill sprigs and serve immediately.

2 large ripe **avocados**
1 cup **plain yogurt**
juice of 2 **limes**

avocado and lime smoothie

1 Cut 8 small chunks from the avocados and set aside.

2 Peel the remaining avocados, remove the pits and roughly chop the flesh.

3 Place the flesh in a blender with the yogurt and the lime juice. Blend until smooth then pour into 4 glasses.

4 Garnish with the reserved chunks of avocado and serve immediately.

1 cup **water**

2 **green tea bags**

2 cups **plain yogurt**

2 handfuls **spinach**, washed and roughly chopped

1 **red chili**, seeds removed and finely chopped

green tea and spinach smoothie

1 Heat the water to about 160°F and add the tea bags. Let the tea steep for 10 minutes.

2 Remove the tea bags and place the tea in a blender with the yogurt, spinach, and chili. Blend until smooth and serve immediately.

1 large **cucumber**

1 **soft lettuce**, shredded

½ small **honeydew melon**, peeled and seeds removed

2 **nectarines**, pits removed

cucumber, lettuce, and honeydew melon smoothie

1 Cut wedges off the cucumber for the garnish and set aside.

2 Roughly chop the remaining cucumber and place in a blender with the lettuce.

3 Roughly chop the melon and nectarines and place in the blender.

4 Blend until smooth and serve in glasses garnished with the reserved cucumber.

1 large **cucumber**

2½ oz **arugula**

2 cups **plain yogurt**

arugula and cucumber smoothie

1 Using a vegetable peeler, cut 4 thin strips of cucumber lengthways and thread them onto wooden skewers for the garnish.

2 Remove the seeds from the cucumber and roughly chop the flesh.

3 Place the flesh in a blender with the arugula and yogurt and blend until smooth.

4 Serve in glasses garnished with the skewered cucumber.

2 large **bananas**
3 cups **plain yogurt**
6 tbsp **caramel syrup**
2 **ice cubes**
4 tbsp **chopped nuts**

banana and caramel smoothie

1 Place the bananas, yogurt, syrup, and ice cubes in a blender and blend until smooth.

2 Pour into glasses, garnish with the chopped nuts and serve.

MAKES 4 servings   **PREP TIME** 15 min   **DIFFICULTY** easy

2 **mangoes**, peeled and pits removed
2 **passion fruit**
2 **bananas**, roughly chopped
18 oz **plain yogurt**
2 **ice cubes**

tropical fruit smoothie

1 Cut 4 small slices from the mangoes to use as decoration and roughly chop the remaining flesh.

2 Scrape the seeds and juice from the passion fruit and set half aside for the decoration. Place the remainder in a blender with the chopped mangoes, bananas, yogurt, and ice and blend until smooth.

MAKES 4 servings   **PREP TIME** 10 min   **DIFFICULTY** easy

9 oz **strawberries**
2 cups **plain yogurt**
1 **banana**, roughly chopped
⅔ cup **acai berry juice**

acai berry and strawberry smoothie

1 Take 4 strawberries, cut each in half and thread onto wooden skewers for the decoration.

2 Remove the hulls from the remaining strawberries and place them in a blender with the remaining ingredients.

3 Blend until smooth, pour into glasses and serve decorated with the skewered strawberries.

1 **mango**, peeled, pit removed and roughly chopped

2 **bananas**, roughly chopped

2 cups **plain yogurt**

6 **ice cubes**

banana and mango smoothie

1 Place all the ingredients in a blender, blend until smooth and serve immediately.

2 **peaches**, pitted and chopped

3 handfuls **blueberries**

2 handfuls **spinach**, chopped

½ cups **apple juice**

ice cubes

peach, blueberry, and spinach smoothie

1 Mix all the ingredients in a blender and blend till you have a smooth texture.

2 Pour into 4 glasses.

1 large handful **sea buckthorn**

1 **mango**, peeled, pit removed, and cubed

1 **banana**

1 ½ cups **coconut milk**

2 tbsp **honey**

ice cubes

sea buckthorn smoothie

1 Mix all the ingredients in a blender and blend till you have a smooth texture.

2 Pour into 4 small glasses.

juice of 4 **limes**

leaves from 2 sprigs of **mint**, plus extra sprigs to decorate

4 tbsp **sugar**

1 cup **plain yogurt**

1 handful **ice cubes**

lime smoothie

1 Place the lime juice and mint leaves in a blender and blend until smooth. Pass through a fine sieve then return the juice to the blender.

2 Add the sugar, yogurt, and ice cubes and blend.

3 Pour into glasses, decorate with the mint leaves and serve immediately.

½ small **cantaloupe melon**, peeled, seeds removed and roughly chopped

3 cups **orange juice**

1 cup **plain yogurt**

juice of 1 **lime**

melon and orange smoothie

1 Place all the ingredients in a blender and blend until smooth.

2 Pour into glasses and serve immediately.

3½ oz **blueberries**

3½ oz **raspberries**

5 oz **cherries**, pits removed

2 cups **plain yogurt**

1 **banana**, roughly chopped

1 cup **orange juice**

cherry and berry smoothie

1 Set aside a few of the berries for the decoration and place the remainder in a blender with the cherries, yogurt, banana, and orange juice.

2 Blend until smooth then pour into 4 glasses and decorate with the reserved berries.

⅞ cup **chocolate and hazelnut spread**

2 cups **plain yogurt**

½ cup **milk**

2 **bananas**, roughly chopped

1 oz **dark chocolate**, grated

banana and chocolate smoothie

1 Put the chocolate spread in a blender with the yogurt, milk, and bananas.

2 Blend until smooth then pour into glasses and sprinkle with the grated chocolate.

¼ small **honeydew melon**, peeled and seeds removed

small bunch **parsley**, roughly chopped, plus extra to decorate

2 sprigs **mint**, roughly chopped

juice of 2 **limes**

12 **ice cubes**

honeydew melon and parsley smoothie

1 Roughly chop the melon and put it in a blender with the parsley, mint, lime juice, and ice cubes.

2 Blend until smooth and slushy then pour into glasses and decorate with a sprig of parsley.

1 cup **pineapple juice**

1 cup **coconut milk**

1 cup **plain yogurt**

2 **bananas**

2 **passion fruit**

calypso passion fruit smoothie

1 Place the pineapple juice, coconut milk, yogurt, and bananas in a blender and blend until smooth.

2 Pour into glasses then cut open the passion fruit, scoop out the seeds and flesh with a spoon and drop into the smoothies. Serve immediately.

7 oz **cherries**, pits removed

2 **bananas**

3 cups **plain yogurt**

chocolate drops, to decorate

banana and cherry smoothie

1 Place the cherries, bananas, and yogurt in a blender and blend until smooth.

2 Pour into glasses, sprinkle over the chocolate drops and serve immediately.

3 cups **mango juice**

2 **bananas**

5 oz **strawberries**

mint leaves, to decorate

fruit smoothie

1 Place the mango juice, bananas, and strawberries in a blender and blend until smooth.

2 Pour into glasses and serve decorated with the mint leaves.

7 **passion fruit**

3 cups **plain yogurt**

2 **bananas**

juice of 1 **lime**

passion fruit smoothie

1 Scoop the seeds and flesh from one of the passion fruits and set aside.

2 Scoop the seeds and flesh from the remaining passion fruits and place in a blender with the yogurt, bananas, and lime juice.

3 Pour the smoothies into glasses and top with the reserved passion fruit seeds and flesh.

MAKES 4 servings   **PREP TIME** 5 min   **DIFFICULTY** easy

¼ **watermelon**, peeled and chopped into chunks
3 **kiwis**, peeled
1 handful **strawberries**
ice cubes

watermelon and kiwi smoothie

1 Mix all the ingredients in a blender and blend till you have a smooth texture.

2 Pour into glasses.

2 handfuls **blueberries**

½ in **fresh ginger**, peeled

1 **banana**

1 ½ cups **vanilla soy milk**

blueberry and ginger smoothie

1 Mix all the ingredients in a blender and blend till you have a smooth texture.

2 Pour into glasses.

3 cups **plain yogurt**

2 **bananas**

5 oz **blueberries**

purple sugar sprinkles, to decorate

banana and berry smoothie

1 Place the yogurt, bananas, and blueberries in a blender and blend until smooth.

2 Pour into glasses and top with the sugar sprinkles.

3 **bananas**

juice of 1 **lemon**

2 **green apples**, peeled, cored and roughly chopped

3 cups **plain yogurt**

4 **ice cubes**

banana and apple smoothie

1 Slice the bananas, coat 8 slices in a little of the lemon juice and thread onto wooden skewers. Set aside for the decoration.

2 Place the remaining ingredients into a blender and blend until smooth. Pour into glasses and serve with the skewered banana slices.

MAKES 4 servings   PREP TIME 5 min   DIFFICULTY easy

2 cups **cranberry juice**
1 cup **plain yogurt**
3 ½ oz **raspberries**
3 ½ oz **blueberries**
1 **banana**
8 **ice cubes**

berry smoothie

1 Place the cranberry juice, yogurt, berries, and banana into a blender and blend until smooth.

2 Pour into glasses, add the ice cubes and serve immediately.

7 oz **blueberries**

1 small **banana**

1⅓ cups **plain yogurt**

mint leaves, to decorate

blueberry smoothie

1 Place half the blueberries in a blender with the banana and yogurt and blend until smooth.

2 Pour into glasses and decorate with the remaining blueberries and the mint leaves.

2 **bananas**

2 cups **orange juice**

2 cups **plain yogurt**

orange slices, to decorate

grated nutmeg, to decorate

banana and orange yogurt smoothie

1 Put the bananas, orange juice, and yogurt in a blender and blend until smooth.

2 Pour into glasses and serve decorated with the orange slices and grated nutmeg.

9 oz **cherries**, pits removed

1¾ oz **sugar**

½ cup **water**

1 cup **plain yogurt**

1 cup **coconut milk**

cherries, to decorate

cherry smoothie with coconut milk

1 Put the cherries in a small pan with the sugar and water and gently heat, stirring from time to time, until the sugar has dissolved.

2 Simmer for 10 minutes then leave to cool for 10 minutes.

3 Press the mixture through a sieve. Reserve about 2 tablespoons of the juice then put the remaining juice in a blender with the yogurt and coconut milk.

4 Blend until smooth then pour into glasses. Swirl the reserved juice on top of the smoothies, decorate with cherries and serve immediately.

4 large **carrots** or 1½ cups **carrot juice**

1½ cups **apple juice**

1 **banana**

carrot batons, to garnish

watercress, to garnish

carrot smoothie

1 Pass the carrots through a vegetable juicer, or put the carrot juice in a blender with the apple juice and banana and blend until smooth.

2 Serve the smoothie garnished with carrot batons and watercress.

7 oz **raspberries**
2 cups **plain yogurt**
½ cup **apple juice**
1 **banana**
ice cubes
mint leaves, to decorate

berry and mint smoothie

1 Place the raspberries, yogurt, apple juice, banana, and ice in a blender and blend until smooth.

2 Pour into glasses and serve garnished with the mint leaves.

4 **passion fruit**

juice from 2 **blood oranges**

2½ oz **blueberries**

2 cups **plain yogurt**

1 **banana**

2 tbsp **crème fraîche**

blood orange and passion fruit smoothie

1 Scoop out the seeds and flesh from the passion fruit and set aside 1 tablespoon for the decoration.

2 Put the remaining passion fruit seeds and flesh in a blender with the orange juice, blueberries, yogurt, and banana.

3 Blend until smooth then pour into glasses. Top with the crème fraîche and the reserved passion fruit and serve immediately.

5 **blood oranges**, peeled and roughly chopped

2 tbsp **mint leaves**

1 handful **strawberries**

ice cubes

mint and blood orange smoothie ✳

1 Mix all the ingredients in a blender and blend till you have a smooth texture.

2 Pour into glasses.

4 tbsp **sugar**

1 tsp **vanilla essence**

juice of 1 **lemon**

½ tbsp **lemon peel**

2½ cups **buttermilk**

Danish buttermilk and lemon smoothie

1 Whisk together the sugar, vanilla, and lemon juice.

2 Add the lemon peel and buttermilk.

3 Leave to infuse in fridge for 30 minutes.

7 oz **strawberries**, roughly chopped
1 cup **red grape juice**
2 cups **apple juice**
1 **banana**
6 **ice cubes**

strawberry, apple, and grape smoothie

1 Place all the ingredients in a blender and blend until smooth.

2 Pour into glasses and serve immediately.

1¾ oz **shredded coconut**

2 cups **plain yogurt**

5 oz **strawberries**

7 tbsp **coconut cream**

1 **banana**

strawberry shortcake smoothie with coconut

1 In a dry pan, toast the shredded coconut until lightly browned then set aside.

2 Place the remaining ingredients in a blender and blend until smooth.

3 Pour into glasses and serve with the toasted coconut sprinkled on top.

1 **cucumber**, peeled, seeds removed and roughly chopped

1 **avocado**, peeled and pit removed

2 cups **plain yogurt**

4 **kiwi fruit**, peeled and roughly chopped

cucumber, avocado, and kiwi smoothie

1 Place all the ingredients in a blender and blend until smooth.

2 Pour into glasses and serve immediately.

MAKES 4 servings   **PREP TIME** 10 min   **DIFFICULTY** easy

5 oz **smooth peanut butter**, plus more to decorate

5 oz **strawberries**

2 cups **plain yogurt**

½ cup **milk**

1 **banana**

peanut butter and strawberry smoothie

1 Place all the ingredients in a blender and blend until smooth.

2 Pour into glasses and serve with a spoonful of peanut butter on top.

1 **mango**, peeled, pit removed and flesh roughly chopped

2 **bananas**

3 cups **plain yogurt**

4 tbsp **granola** or **muesli**

mango and banana smoothie

1 Place the mango, bananas, and yogurt in a blender and blend until smooth.

2 Pour into glasses and scatter the granola or muesli on top. Serve immediately.

2 medium **dragon fruit**, peeled and roughly chopped
1 lb 10 oz **watermelon**, peeled, seeds removed and roughly chopped
1 cup **plain yogurt**
4 tbsp **honey**

dragon fruit and
watermelon smoothie

1 Place all the ingredients in a blender and blend until smooth.

2 Pour into glasses and serve.

3 **bananas**

juice of 1 **lemon**

2 **green apples**, peeled, cored, and roughly chopped

3 cups **plain yogurt**

4 **ice cubes**

banapple smoothie

1 Slice the bananas, coat 8 slices in a little of the lemon juice and thread onto wooden skewers. Set aside.

2 Place the remaining ingredients into a blender and blend until smooth. Pour into glasses and serve with the skewered banana slices.

MAKES 4 servings   PREP TIME 15 min   DIFFICULTY easy

5 **green figs**
½ small **soft lettuce**
18 oz **watermelon**, peeled, seeds removed and roughly chopped
2 large **peaches**, pits removed and roughly chopped
1 cup **water**

fig and lettuce smoothie

1 Cut one of the figs into 4 wedges and set aside.

2 Put the remaining ingredients into a blender and blend until smooth.

3 Pour into glasses and serve garnished with the fig wedges.

1 punnet **cress**

1 bunch **radishes**, trimmed

1 tsp **horseradish** (freshly grated or from a jar)

juice of ½ **lemon**

3 cups cold **buttermilk**

radish and cress milk

1 Cut a little of the cress and set aside for the garnish.

2 Place the remaining cress in a blender with the rest of the ingredients and blend until smooth.

3 Season with salt and pepper and serve garnished with the reserved cress.

2 **assam or ceylon tea bags**

2½ cups **water**

sugar, to taste

1 **cinnamon stick**

2 slices **fresh ginger**

4 **cloves**

4 **peppercorns**

2 **star anise**

1½ cups **orange juice**

ice cubes

1 **orange**, sliced

spiced orange iced tea

1 Boil the tea bags in the water with the sugar and all the spices. Leave to cool. Strain the liquid after chilling.

2 Pour the mixture into a large pitcher and top up with orange juice, ice cubes, and orange slices.

3 If you prefer a frappé, then mix all ingredients apart from orange slices in a blender and blend till you have a smooth texture.

4 Pour into glasses.

1 tbsp **almonds**

1 tbsp **pumpkin seeds**

1 tbsp **sunflower seeds**

1 tbsp **flaxseed**

2 cups **soy milk**

1 **banana**

4 tbsp **maple syrup**

2 handfuls **blueberries**

6 tbsp of your favorite **granola**

"rise and shine" breakfast smoothie

1 Mix all the ingredients in a blender and blend till you have a smooth texture.

2 Pour into glasses and sprinkle the granola on top.

14 oz **pineapple**, peeled and roughly chopped

1 **cucumber**, roughly chopped

4 tbsp **mint leaves**

ice cubes

pineapple, cucumber, and mint smoothie

1 Using a vegetable peeler, cut thin strips of cucumber lengthways and set aside.

2 Mix all the remaining ingredients in a blender and blend till you have a smooth texture.

3 Pour into glasses and garnish with the cucumber strips.

4 small **peaches**, pitted and chopped

2 handfuls **raspberries**

2 cups **plain yogurt**

ice cubes

peach melba smoothie

1 Mix all the ingredients in a blender and blend till you have a smooth texture.

2 Pour into glasses.

6 tbsp **blanched almonds**

12 **apricots** (fresh or dried), chopped

4 tbsp **honey**

2½ cups regular **soy milk**

ice cubes

almond and apricot smoothie

1 Mix all the ingredients in a blender and blend till you have a smooth texture.

2 Pour into glasses and serve with spoon.

6 tbsp **oats** soaked in ½ cup **apple juice** for 10–15 minutes

2 tbsp **hazelnuts**, plus 1 tbsp chopped and toasted **hazelnuts**

2 **bananas**

2 cups **soy milk**

ice cubes

oats, hazelnuts, banana, and soy smoothie

1 Mix the oats, nuts, bananas, soy milk and ice cubes in a blender and blend till you have a smooth texture.

2 Pour into glasses and sprinkle with toasted hazelnuts.

2 chamomile tea bags

2 cups **water**

2 **peaches**, pitted and roughly chopped

½ in **fresh ginger**, peeled

4 tbsp **honey**

ice cubes

chamomile, peach, and ginger iced tea

1 Make a pot of strongly brewed chamomile tea with the tea bags and water, then chill until it is tepid.

2 Mix all the ingredients in a blender and blend till you have a smooth texture.

3 Pour into glasses.

2 tsp **matcha green tea powder**

2 **avocados**, pitted and roughly chopped

1 cup **apple juice**

1½ cups **plain yogurt**

ice cubes

matcha and avocado smoothie

1 Mix all the ingredients in a blender and blend till you have a smooth texture.

2 Pour into glasses.

4 small **peaches**, chopped

1½ cups **almond milk**

4 tbsp **sugar syrup**

1 tbsp **almonds**

pinch of **ground cinnamon**

ice cubes

peach, cinnamon, and almond milk smoothie

1 Mix all ingredients in a blender and blend till you have a smooth texture.

2 handfuls **blueberries**

1 cup **orange juice**

½ cups **plain yogurt**

blueberry and orange smoothie

1 Mix all the ingredients in a blender and blend till you have a smooth texture.

2 Pour into glasses.

1 ½ handfuls **raspberries**

1 ½ handfuls **strawberries**

3 tbsp **lime juice**

ice cubes

1–2 tbsp **sugar syrup**, to taste (optional)

strawberries, to decorate

raspberry, lime, and strawberry smoothie

1 Mix all the ingredients in a blender and blend till you have a smooth texture.

2 Pour into glasses and decorate each with a strawberry.

6 scoops **grapefruit sorbet**

1½ cups **blood orange juice**

½ cup **passion fruit syrup**

mint leaves, to decorate

grapefruit and blood orange smoothie

1 Mix all the ingredients in a blender and blend till you have a smooth texture.

2 Pour into glasses and decorate with the mint leaves.

3-day juice detox

3-day juice detox

An unbalanced diet, irregular eating, and over-consumption of sugar, combined with a high intake of nicotine, alcohol, or caffeine, all affect our looks and our wellbeing. If you've subjected your body to irregular mealtimes, ready-made foods and all too many toxins over the years, it will thank you for a detox. Try a three-day juice detox and by the end of it you'll feel full of energy and wellbeing—and years younger.

When the body gets rid of toxins, it also sheds superfluous liquid, helping you to kick-start your new lifestyle. The best way to ensure a healthy and safe weight loss is to establish good eating habits, as well as doing a detox once in a while. Don't put yourself through a long cure, one to three days is more than enough, especially the first few times you try it.

A juice fast can help to gently cleanse your body, and will also help your body restore its alkaline balance and normalize your digestion and metabolism. In this three-day doet we have suggested ingredients that will kick-start the detox process and which will stimulate both your digestion and your immune system.

some potential benefits of a juice detox are:

- Clearer skin
- Regular bowels
- The kidneys and liver become more efficient
- Reduces stress, balances hormones, and eases inflammations
- Strengthens the immune system
- Gives you lots of energy and mental clarity

If there's one thing you should know before you embark on a detox, it's that preparation is the key to success. The changes will come more easily, and you'll feel better much quicker, the more prepared you are. How you prepare your body will affect how you feel and how your body will respond to the cure.

The first detox symptoms will disappear quite fast, if you're well prepared. A couple of days before you start the diet, cut down on coffee, sugar, meat, and dairy products. Make sure you eat fresh fruits and vegetables with every meal. Timing is also essential. A good time to detox is when you know you that you'll be able to focus on yourself. Don't attempt a detox cure if you know you'll have a hectic week at work. Think about your pre-detox plan as a way to get your body in harmony—you will thank yourself when you're doing the actual detox.

so, here's your three-day cure:

Start each day with a glass of water with a good squeeze of lemon juice. This will help cleanse your kidneys.

juice 1: a slightly sweet juice, makes the perfect breakfast.

juice 2: is a filling juice at lunchtime to pep you up for the afternoon.

juice 3: at mid-afternoon will stabilize the blood sugar levels.

juice 4: drunk before bed, will help you settle for the night.

4 thick wedges **watermelon**, peeled
2 handfuls **strawberries**

juice 1: **sweet start**

Rich in zinc and potassium, which helps the body to get rid of toxins.

1 Juice the fruits.

2 Put the juice in a blender together with a couple of ice cubes and blend. Pour into a glass.

4 **apples**

4 **carrots**, halved

juice 1: **apples and carrots**

Rich in zinc and potassium, which helps the body to get rid of toxins.

1 Juice the apples and carrots.

2 Put the juice in a blender together with a couple of ice cubes and blend. Pour into a glass.

2 handfuls **blackberries**

1 small **pineapple**, peeled and roughly chopped

juice 1: blue dream

Pineapple contains bromelain, which eases muscle tension, while blackberries are a good source of folic acid.

1 Juice the blackberries first, and then continue with the pineapple, so that the pulp goes through the juicer.

2 Put the juice in a blender together with a couple of ice cubes and blend. Pour into a glass.

4 **carrots**

4 **celery stalks**

3 handfuls **spinach**

3 handfuls **lettuce/salad**

1 small handful **parsley**

juice 2: the great green

Removes toxins from the liver and the lymphatic system, and protects from serious illness.

1 Juice all the ingredients, putting the spinach, lettuce, and parsley between the other vegetables.

2 Put the juice in a blender together with a couple of ice cubes and blend. Pour into a glass.

2 **carrots**

½ **green pepper**, deseeded

1 small handful **spinach**

½ small **onion**, peeled

3 **celery stalks**

½ **cucumber**

1 medium-sized **tomato**

juice 2: **super seven**

Real energy booster, with health benefits galore!

1 Juice all the ingredients and season with salt and pepper. Pour into a glass.

MAKES 1 serving   **PREP TIME** 10 min   **DIFFICULTY** easy

4 **pineapple wedges**, peeled

1 small handful **grapes**

½ **orange**, peeled

½ **apple**

½ **mango**, pit removed and chopped

1 **banana**

juice 3: sweet success

This juice is full of complex carbohydrates, keeping your energy levels up during the detox.

1 Juice the pineapple, grapes, oranges, and apples.

2 Mix the juice and a couple of ice cubes with the mango and the banana in a blender, until you get a sweet and delicious smoothie. Pour into a glass.

1 **grapefruit**, peeled

2 **kiwi fruits**, peeled

¼ **pineapple**, peeled and roughly chopped

1 small handful **frozen raspberries**

1 small handful **frozen cranberries**

juice 3: **winds of change**

A crisp and clean juice, full of vitamin A and C, selenium, and zinc.

1 Juice the grapefruit, kiwis, and pineapple.

2 Mix the juice and the frozen berries in a blender. Pour into a glass.

6 **carrots**

4 **figs**

2 **oranges**, peeled

2 in **fresh ginger**, peeled and halved

2 **bananas**

juice 4: good night

Bananas and figs are high in tryptophan. Tryptophan is necessary for the production of serotonin, which gives a feeling of wellbeing. These fruits contain a lot of natural sugar, so they give a sensation of satisfaction and can prevent you feeling hungry.

1 Juice the carrots, figs, oranges, and ginger.

2 Pour the juice into a blender and mix it with banana and 2 ice cubes for 20 seconds, until you get a delicious smoothie. Pour into a glass.

¼ **pineapple**, peeled

1½ handfuls **grapes**

2 large handfuls **lettuce/salad**

3 **celery stalks**

juice 4: **sweet dreams**

Pineapple and grapes boost your blood sugar levels, aiding sleep. Salad and celery encourage your nerves and muscles to relax.

1 Juice all the ingredients. Pour into a glass.

index

Photo Credits

The photography in this book was provided by Catrine Mannerup,
Kate Kamil and Stockfood Ltd.

Please see www.pulpmedia.co.uk for further information